I0797821

The Water Remedy

The Water Remedy

Folklore, ritual and wisdom

Clare Gogerty

2025

© Clare Gogerty, 2025

All rights reserved. No part of this book may be reproduced in any material form (including photocopying or storing it in any medium by electronic means and whether or not transiently or incidentally to some other use of this publication) without the written permission of the copyright owner. Applications for the copyright owner's written permission to reproduce any part of this publication should be addressed to Calon, University Registry, King Edward VII Avenue, Cardiff CF10 3NS.

www.uwp.co.uk

British Library Cataloguing-in-Publication Data
A catalogue record for this book is available from the British Library.

ISBN: 978-1-83760-002-1

The right of Clare Gogerty to be identified as author of this work has been asserted in accordance with sections 77 and 79 of the Copyright, Designs and Patents Act 1988.

For GPSR enquiries please contact: Easy Access System Europe
Oü, 16879218. Mustam.e tee 50, 10621, Tallinn, Estonia.
gpsr.requests@easproject.com

Cover design by Andy Ward
Typeset by Agnes Graves
Printed in Great Britain by Bell & Bain Ltd, Glasgow

Contents

Introduction

The Source of All Things

'Water is the driving force of all nature...
In time and with water,
everything changes.'
Leonardo da Vinci

My parents were born and raised in Ebbw Vale, a steel town in the south Wales valleys. When young, my father worked in the steelworks, but he was a romantic and a wanderer at heart, and he headed for the hills or the sea whenever he could to hike and to fish. The village of Llangynidr, where the Usk is wide and fast flowing, was one of his favourite haunts. The eighteenth-century bridge is notable for its age and its six arches, which step across the rushing river, and its miniature waterfalls that ripple over the stony riverbed. It is easy to see why my father was drawn to this place and why he took my mother there to ask her to marry him – and why she accepted. Who could resist a bearded romantic proffering a ring in such a lovely spot?

Shortly after they got married, they moved to Canada, where my brother and I were born. Although we lived in the centre of Toronto, no opportunity was missed to head out to the lakes or to Niagara Falls. Photographs at this time show us all lined up in waterproofs beneath the Falls, or sitting in a rowing boat on a lake with a fishing line trailing optimistically behind. Later, we returned to Wales where bank holidays saw the four of us sitting in traffic on the way to the

Pembrokeshire coast or Barry Island, the boot packed with picnic hampers, rugs and swimsuits.

These days I live in the depths of rural Herefordshire, about as far from the sea as it is possible to get. Water is all around, though, beneath our feet in underground aquifers and running through the village in a brook, before pooling in a lake. The orchard here has a stream running alongside it, which is fed by a cool, clear spring. The water rushes along over bumpy stones on its way to join the village brook, much like the Usk did at Llangyndir all those years ago when my parents were beginning their life together. My father's life has ended but the river still flows, carrying with it our family memories and those of countless others who have been drawn to it.

Water stories thread, stream-like, through all our lives.

Many of our best memories are made in or near water: paddling in the sea; swimming in a river; picnicking by a mountain lake; cooling hot wrists or gulping water from a fountain. The pull of water is irresistible; we are drawn to it, not just because without it we would not survive, but because of its beauty and because it is a source of healing and wellbeing.

Water in its many forms invites us to look at it, whether it's the rolling heave of the ocean or the hurried coursing of a stream. We often head to a riverbank or a canal path when the urge to go for a walk arises. Children and dogs automatically run towards water and instinctively know how to play in it. For most adults, there are few things as refreshing as standing by the invigorating force of a waterfall, and fewer as joyful as a dip in the ocean. The movement, colour and sound of water soothes and heals; it makes shoulders drop and breathing quieten.

Although water provides the setting for some of our most memorable experiences, our treatment of it is decidedly casual. It is the backdrop to our lives, running through the landscape and our bodies, keeping humans and animals alive, and nourishing crops and forests, yet we largely ignore it. We often even forget to drink.

We rarely think about how easily it comes out of our taps or where it goes when it drains away. Like good health, we take it for granted when we have it and mourn it when we don't. Ask most people where their water comes from, and they can't answer. Many only consider its importance when their families or homes are threatened or destroyed by flooding, or when drought makes life barely possible.

It is a much-quoted statistic that our bodies are composed largely of water: around 70–80 per cent. We are constantly told to drink more of it to maintain good health, specifically to keep blood running freely, but even so we forget to drink. Which is a mistake, as even mild dehydration can affect mental performance, with headaches being the first manifestation of a lack of water. A healthy human can live for a month without food but will die in less than a week without fresh water.

Our ancestors, however, were more in touch with water; as they actively had to seek it out, they worshipped and respected this magical fluid and its life-giving properties. Unlike us, spoilt by modern convenience, and at the mercy of water companies driven by profit rather than water health, they had to find it, carry it and store it. The same is true, of course, in countries where fresh water is already scarce and growing increasingly so. According to the non-profit organisation One Drop (www.onedrop.org), 2 billion people globally lack safe drinking water, and 291 million people spend more than thirty minutes per round trip collecting it. When our forebears found a water source, especially if it was a pure, cold spring gushing from the ground, it felt like a gift sent directly from the gods. The Celts were particularly fascinated by water's powers of nourishment, healing, cleansing, regeneration and destruction. Numerous water deities presiding over rivers, streams, lakes and wells were worshipped in pre-Christian Britain. Many of these were female; water is linked to the moon after all, a female force that governs the tides and women's cycles. Folklore, myths and legends are full of tales of enchanted wells, mermaids, sea deities, ladies of the lake and green-teethed swamp creatures.

The sanctity of water goes back even further: Greek philosophers described it as one of the four elements that made up the universe (the others being fire, earth and air). Water is also one of the five elements in traditional Chinese philosophy (along with earth, fire, wood and metal). Most religions have a long history of water purifications ceremonies – ritual washing or total body immersion occur in Christianity, Hinduism, Islam, Judaism, the Rastafari movement, Shinto and Taoism. For many indigenous people of the Americas, water is central to their belief system – it does not just sustain life, but it is sacred. In the 2017 protest to stop the building of a pipeline beneath the Missouri River in North Dakota, the Lakota phrase, '*Mní wičhóni*' ('water is life') was chanted by protestors: a clear indication of the value they placed on it. Water also plays a central role in the creation mythology of the Kogi tribe of Sierra Nevada, in Colombia: in the beginning there was only the sea, and the sea was the Mother who gave birth to the world. There are many other examples of the reverence shown by Native Americans: the Koyukon people of Alaska, for example, define cardinal directions not in terms of north and south but as upstream and downstream, while the Blackfeet viewed the water as the home of divine beings and animals.

Bodies of water continue to be venerated worldwide, and attract large numbers of pilgrims seeking healing, purification and transformation. Christian mythology, for instance, suggests that the Chalice Well at Glastonbury in Somerset, England, is where the vessel that caught Christ's blood was brought by Joseph of Arimathea. The grotto at Lourdes in France, where a young woman called Bernadette saw a vision of the Virgin Mary pointing to a spring, is a place of healing and prayer for Catholics. Crater Lake in Oregon, USA, considered a portal to the underworld, was so sacred to the Klamath people that for a long time it was only visited by shaman and chiefs.

The Ganges River in India is the living embodiment of the goddess Ganga for Hindus. According to Hindu mythology, the goddess Ganga descended from the heavens in Lord Shiva's hair, then was released in streams that became the river. Its holy status means that there are many temples along its riverbanks dedicated to Ganga, and Hindus believe that its waters have the power to cleanse and purify sins. Pilgrims continue to bathe in the Ganges despite it being one of the most polluted rivers on Earth. The world's biggest spiritual gathering, the Kumbh Mela, takes place at the confluence of the Ganges, Yamuna and mythical Sarasvati rivers once every four years. (For more on confluences, see page 58.)

These days most of us are propelled to visit a body of water not by a religious directive but by instinct. We walk to a lake or river, dip our hands in a well, or drive to the sea to shift our mood or state of mind, knowing that water can rejuvenate, calm and invigorate.

Water, Water Everywhere

Although we often feel calmed by water and go in search of it for solace and peace, the hydrologic (water) cycle is anything but calm. All is movement, from the flex of freeze and thaw that turns mountains into sand, to enormous aquifers beneath our feet that ooze water slowly through the ground.

How the same amount of water, constantly present on Earth, circulates around the planet is a complex business, but in simple terms, the hydrologic cycle consists of three phases: evaporation, condensation and precipitation. This is an eternal process of rainwater recycling: water falls from the clouds, eventually evaporates on the earth, then rises to form clouds that release new rain. The atmosphere around Earth carries only about a ten-day supply of fresh water, about 3 cm of rain. Each day on Earth almost 250 cubic miles of water evaporates into the sea and the land. Its stay in the air is short, as it is always seeking new particles to stick to and fall with as rain or snow.

Water's Continuing Mysteries

'Water is H_2O
Hydrogen two parts
Oxygen one
But there is also a third thing
That makes it water
And nobody knows what that is.'
D. H. Lawrence

Water continues to amaze and baffle in equal measure. There is still much we don't know about this seemingly uncomplicated and omnipresent element. Many people have studied water to try to understand it better and have come up with a range of theories: Gerald H. Pollack, professor of Bioengineering at the University of Washington, suggests that it does not just exist in the three established forms – solid, liquid and gas – but has another, fourth, phase. This 'ordered', liquid-crystalline phase occurs next to water-loving surfaces and exists almost everywhere. The discovery of it, he suggests in his book, *The Fourth Phase of Water: beyond solid, liquid and vapor*, explains many baffling anomalies, including why our joints work without squeaking, why feather clouds are puffy and white, and how a Jesus Christ lizard can walk on water.

Less scientific, and often disputed, studies have also been carried out, and they suggest that water holds a 'secret intelligence' and responds to human consciousness. Dr Masaru Emoto, an author and alternative healer from Japan, photographed the crystalline structure of frozen water after 'treating' it with positive or negative statements, playing classical music to it and blessing it. He found the structure of the crystals differed according to the treatment: positive samples created pleasingly symmetrical structures; negative samples created asymmetrical ones. He published the results in a best-selling, but controversial, book: *The Hidden Messages in Water*.

Veda Austin, a water researcher and author, takes Emoto's research with ice crystals further. She communicates with water through words, thoughts and pictures, then takes macroscopic photographs of the ice crystals formed during a stage between liquid and ice, which she calls a 'state of creation'. In her books, *The Secret Intelligence of Water* and *The Living Language of Water*, she reveals that the result is patterns that echo what she communicated – for example, a photograph of a girl's plait was 'copied' by adjacent ice crystals. If we think water has an intelligence, she says, we will once more regard it as living and sacred, and take better care of it.

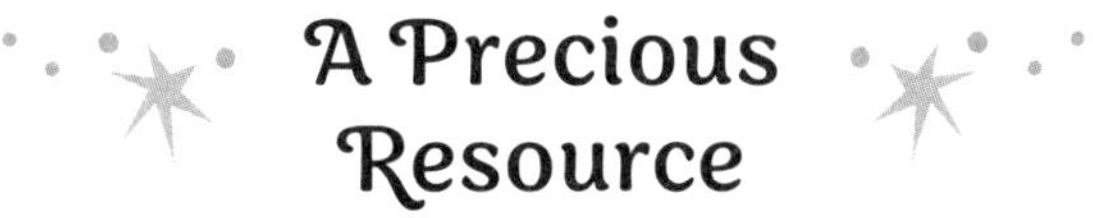

A Precious Resource

Research leading to a greater understanding of water can only be a good thing. The more we know about it, the more we can protect it. Despite its abundance, due to our mismanagement of it, water grows more precious every day, with the most urgent demand being in our homes. Which is why the current critical shortage of clean, fresh water is a developing catastrophe. The problem is not that we have too little of it – Earth has virtually the same amount of water as it has always had (97 per cent of that is salt water; 3 per cent is fresh water; and two-thirds is ice). The issue is how this limited resource is used and abused. The reckless withdrawal of fresh surface and ground water has led to a critical depletion of aquifers, which – alongside pollution of rivers and lakes – has created a severe lack of clean water. This, combined with the effects of climate change, threatens our coasts, marine life and future generations of life on Earth.

Water moves. If you have something you don't want, water will take it away. As a result, it carries a large amount of stuff that floats, dissolves or is suspended by it. This movement – its beauty, its support of life – makes it the single most recreational resource on Earth but also leads to its contamination by pollutants.

Despite this gloomy state of affairs, there is some hope for our water supply. Concerned conservationists are restoring streams and lakes, as well as reintroducing salmon fry, beavers and other wild creatures. Meanders, floodplains and rivers clogged by erosion or channelled inappropriately for housing developments are being helped back to health. Growing awareness of pollution of rivers and seas has prompted a groundswell of angry citizens demanding that better care is taken of this precious resource.

It is time to make like our ancestors and treat water with the respect it deserves. My aim for this book is to write an appreciation of water in all its forms – a prompt to us all to take more care of it – and in the process suggest ways to work with it to boost our own wellbeing. A responsible appreciation of water is fundamental to our ecological, environmental and spiritual values. It is time to honour the spirits of water.

Chapter One

Deep Water

Sacred springs, holy wells

'Where a spring rises or a water flows,
there ought we to build altars
and offer sacrifices.'
Roman philosopher Seneca

I am fortunate to have a well of my own, although this is not unusual in my village, as a stream runs through it to a substantial brook in the valley below. Many wells and pumps tap into to the stream on its journey, and although they were once the main water supply, now they are used to water gardens and fill ponds. My well is inside the house – when the house was extended, the well was covered with a thick glass sheet and a new structure, a kitchen, was built around it. Water is pumped from the well to a tap in the garden. Originally, it would have been the sole source of water for the household, but now I use it to water my pots and fill the pond. The well is one of the reasons I bought the house; having it felt lucky, a blessing.

Although I have always appreciated it, I had initially regarded the well simply as a useful additional water supply – until, that is, I had a visit from Gordon Field, artist, tree guardian and dowser. While many dowsers use their skills to find water (see page 14), Gordon uses his pendulum to source the Earth's energy lines that criss-cross beneath our feet. On arrival at the house, Gordon went immediately to the well. Dowsers' noses always twitch when they are around water and although Gordon's main interest is communicating with trees and Earth energy, water sources draw him equally. Using a pendulum, he dowsed the well and, much to my delight, pronounced it to be a 'beacon well'. He explained that beacon wells are where people once gathered: a coming together of the community not just to collect water, but also to celebrate and give thanks. He was also pleased to report that the well was happy and healthy, and that it had a name: Soersys.

Several weeks later, the local dowsing group came over for a summer gathering in the garden. Kate Smart, who runs the group, suggested that we hold a ceremony over the well to honour the 'goddess of the well' and to express our gratitude for what she provides. Kate brought a few things with her (see ritual, below, for a list) to create a mandala on its glass covering and everyone drew near as she said a few words. It felt appropriate to gather around this 'beacon well' as people had done in the past. It was a moment to acknowledge its presence and its importance, and that of the goddess of the well. (See page 5 for details of the ceremony.)

In participating in this simple and affecting ceremony, we echoed what our ancestors had done around wells all over the world for centuries. Then, of course, water sources were not as readily available as now, and therefore more appreciated.

To our modern eyes, this well water, rising from below the ground, feels like a marvellous surprise. Our ancestors must have thought it was some kind of miracle. As a result, springs were regarded as sacred places of healing imbued with supernatural powers and venerated as such. Now they are mostly overlooked and rarely feature in surveys of ancient monuments, despite being some of the oldest sacred sites in the world. Although they have gradually been forgotten and, in some cases, destroyed, it is reassuring to know that they are still out there, waiting to be found and re-enchanted.

Fortunately, many of the wells that do survive are cherished by local communities and are being rediscovered by a new generation interested in the folkloric past. One of these is the Virtuous Well (aka St Anne's Well) in Trellech (Tryleg), Monmouthshire, in Wales. Trellech has always been a special place; it is also the site of three Bronze Age standing stones, known as Harold's Stones, the site of Tump Turret, formerly a Norman motte and bailey castle, and the medieval church of St Nicholas. It was an important town in the Middle Ages, before falling foul of the Black Death in the fourteenth century and the ravages of the anti-English Welsh military commander Owain Glyndŵr in the fifteenth century.

When I visited the well one crisp spring morning, a party of ramblers sat around it in a companiable huddle, chatting while drinking coffee from flasks. I imagined them as pilgrims who had arrived at their destination, paid their respects and made their offerings, and were now drinking the water fresh from the source, hoping to benefit from its curative powers. The well is a fine, U-shaped stone construction with built-in seats – well suited for such activity. Earlier pilgrims would have travelled miles in the hope of a cure to a variety of illnesses: it is fed by several springs each said to target a different ailment. Legend has it that fairies dance around the well on Midsummer's Eve and, much like teenagers at a party, leave their bluebell drinking cups scattered about post-revelry. The ramblers were more concerned with the vagaries of their route ahead, poring over maps and apps, than the well's healing or supernatural powers, and were soon on their way.

Alone at the well, I walked around it three times in a clockwise (*deosil*) direction. This is a simple ritual that feels good to practise at sacred sites and allows you to approach in a suitably respectful manner. Entering the embracing arms of the stone structure, I walked towards the well, then knelt in front of it, not because of any religious practice but simply to get close to the water. It was not disappointing – it bubbled up thrillingly cold and clear, emerging from the earth in a steady flow, as it had for centuries. I filled a glass jar to take home with me, thanked the well for its enduring benefits, and headed off to find the standing stones.

'Men really know not what good water's worth.
If you had been in Turkey or in Spain,
Or with a famished boat's crew had your berth,
Or in the desert heard the camel's bell,
You'd wish yourself where truth is – in a well.'
From 'Don Juan' by Lord Byron

Springs have been appreciated in all cultures for centuries. They appear from deep beneath the earth, cold and clear, bursting with life, bringing water into the terrestrial realm before starting their journey across the land to the sea. These mysterious water sources embody the power to grow, revive, purify and cleanse. They symbolise the life source itself, delivering that essential element – water – to anyone who needs it.

Countless myths and legends are associated with springs and wells; deities were said to inhabit or guard them, and they were seen as portals to the Otherworld, where fairies and nature spirits frolicked. In the UK, they have been given supernatural powers since pre-Roman times, playing an important part in rituals, and revered equally by witches, diviners, healers and the plain thirsty. Watcr has a long association with fertility and healing, and wells were places of rituals and offerings given in the hope of return favours, such as good health, love and pregnancy.

When the kingdoms of Anglo-Saxon England were converted to Christianity, previously pagan water shrines began to serve the needs of the new religion. Those on a route to another holy place became 'holy wells', with stone structures built around them and their associated pagan deities being 'rebranded' as Christian saints.

Sadly, many wells have fallen into disrepair; they are still bubbling quietly beside churches or hidden in undergrowth at the edges of fields or on street corners, but largely passed by unnoticed. Sacred springs with origins pre-Christianity have no written records and are especially tricky to find, although the quest is always worth it. Wells and springs need to be visited, honoured and thanked – they are the beginning of everything, after all.

How to Approach a Well

Visiting a well is not like visiting any old attraction. It's important not to just rock up, take a photo and dangle your fingers in its water, then leave. Wells should be treated with respect. This is one way to do it.

Set your intention. Think about why you are making the visit: one of the reasons listed below may help. This helps to make the most of your experience.

- When you arrive, approach the well humbly – it is a sacred place and needs to be treated as such. Adopting the pilgrimage practice of circumambulation, i.e. walking around it a few times slowly in a clockwise (*deosil*) direction, is a good way to do this.
- Take some time to get to know it. This can simply be a few minutes sitting beside it, spending a moment in meditation, or something more elaborate, such as a ritual with singing and chanting perhaps.
- Make an offering but keep it natural, i.e. a leaf with a prayer or intention written on it, some water carried from another well, or a pebble taken from your pocket and deposited in its waters. You don't want to leave anything non-biodegradable that will hang around and pollute the space.

A word of warning: if you are heading to a well, be careful of drinking its water unless you are sure it is fit for human consumption. It may well be polluted or be sited downstream from livestock. It's best to pass the water through a filter water bottle first to be on the safe side. Tests are available for sale to check if ground and surface water is free from contamination and is drinkable.

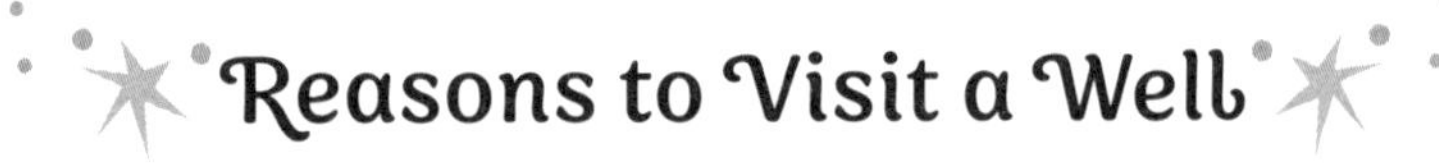

Reasons to Visit a Well

1. To Make A Wish

Years ago, on a tour of sacred sites in Ireland, a group of us went in search of the St Brigid's Well at Castlemagner, in County Cork. The well is on private land, so permission to visit it had been granted by the landowner. The path to reach it took us through woodland, towards a stream, to a fenced area. In front of us, water gurgled from a small, lichen-and-moss-coated stone enclosure, clear, cold, sparkling in the sun. A lintel above the well was inscribed with the name and date of the person who had built the well house (Owen Egan of Knocknanuss, 1787) and on either side of it were two figures: one said to be a *Sile na gig* (a fertility figure of a naked woman with legs spread, also known as a *Sheela-na-gig*) or Brigid herself, and on the other side a male figure, wearing a helmet – possibly St Michael, a Roman centurion or the Devil, depending on who you speak to. Couples having trouble conceiving came here to drink the water and wish for a child; it was also said to cure ailments by applying water-soaked strips of linen to the afflicted part of the body.

Asking watery deities to grant a wish is evident in many wishing wells scattered around the UK. Some of these are roofed wells, with a winched bucket as seen in fairy tales and domestic gardens, but others are on a larger scale, like St Winefride's in Holywell, Wales (see page 18). Throwing coins into a well must be hot-wired into our psyches, because wherever a small body of water exists in a public place – be it a fountain, pool or well – it is lined with glittering coins, each representing someone's secret desire or longing.

Before coins were thrown into wells, pins, often deliberately bent, were frequently used, most likely because they were small, glittery and widely available. They were dropped into St Piran's Well in Cornwall when a child was baptised, for example, and at other wells on a feast day, like Ascension Day or May Day to make a wish. The custom of exchanging a small item in return for the granting a wish goes back to pre-Christian times. It continued with the Romans at sites such as the hot springs at Bath, where wishes were written on small lead tablets and thrown in the water.

That hot summer day in Ireland, we had brought with us simple Brigid's crosses, which we had made from bundles of rush. Brigid is an important Irish saint and, as the figure beside the well might have been her, this felt like the right thing to do. We took it in turns to soak our crosses in the well water and then laid them beside it, each of us making a wish and sending them out to St Brigid via her watery portal.

Well customs to reveal infidelity, uncover a thief and find an absent friend

- Ffynnon Gybi (St Cybi's Well) in Llangybi, Gwynedd, was once an important destination for pilgrims seeking healing, as indicated by the remains of its fine stone buildings and a bathing pool. Visitors also threw rags into the water to assess whether a lover was faithful. If it drifted south, the answer was yes; if it floated north, it was no.
- Nearby at the now neglected Ffynnon Fair (St Mary's Well) in Llanbedrog, Gwynedd, it was believed that the victim of theft could identify a thief by kneeling by the well and 'avow his faith in it', then throwing bread into the water while naming a suspect. If suspicions were correct, the bread would sink. If they weren't, they could have a few more goes until the true culprit was identified.
- In Cornwall, in a field near the church at Gulval, those worried about an absent friend or family member could ask the old woman guardian of the well to intercede on their behalf. If the missing person was alive and well, the still water of the well-pit would bubble up; if they were sick, the water would become foul; if the party was dead, it did none of the above. The well fell into decline when the old woman died and it is now almost impossible to find.

2. To Foretell The Future

To our ancestors, springs were seen as liminal places – portals – inhabited by nature spirits and fairy folk. These ethereal beings were thought to flit between the earthly plane and the underground 'other' world. Springs were seen as places to contact these spirits to ask for wishes to be granted and to predict the future.

Young women with romantic worries headed to the well to find out if they would be resolved happily. (There are no records of young men engaging in a similar activity. Maybe they lacked curiosity.) They would do this by throwing small objects – stones usually – into the water, and then contemplating the bubbles that surfaced. Those wanting to know how many years they had to wait to be married counted them – each represented a year to wait; no bubbles indicated a lifetime of spinsterhood.

3. To Seek Healing

In the days before modern medicine, the sick and injured were drawn to the well by tales of miracles associated with saints offering treatment for their particular ailment. Some of these ailments have almost vanished, thanks to advances in medicine – scurvy, scrofula, distemper, leprosy – while others are still with us and may sound more familiar – rheumatism, 'lameness', warts and 'complaints peculiar to women'. Treatment could involve drinking from the well, possibly accompanied by walking around it several times and making an offering, or total body immersion.

At the larger wells, immersion was the preferred 'cure' for mental health problems, a practice known as 'bowsening' in eastern Cornwall. In the seventeenth century, at St Nonna's Well in Altarnun, near Launceston, the patient was plunged repeatedly and without warning into the icy water of the well until their symptoms were subdued. This was intended to return them to their right frame of mind. Following this freezing and brutal dunking, they were dragged to a nearby church and prayed over. If they hadn't 'returned to their right mind', the whole procedure was repeated until they stopped struggling and it was assumed that they had. Fortunately, this cruel procedure eventually died out, although the bowsening platform remains. Reached by stone steps, surrounded by daffodils and perched above the still water, it is now a place of calm reflection rather than violent subjugation.

Many wells promised healing for poor vision: in Wales several are called *Ffynnon Lygad* (Eye Well). An end to fertility problems was also promised, with some wells credited as having 'a virtue to make women that are barren to bring forth children'. This applied equally to royalty as to the common woman – following a visit to St Agnes Well in Cornwall in 1630, Henrietta Maria, wife of Charles I, became pregnant after having long wished for a child.

Minerals dissolved from surrounding rocks are often credited with giving spring water therapeutic properties, although many springs contain none at all (see page 19). Iron, calcium and magnesium are found in the Chalice Well and White Spring in Glastonbury, for example. The iron helps with anaemia, mental fatigue and the nervous system; the calcium strengthens the bones, muscles and heart, and the magnesium helps muscles relax. Other minerals which manifest as gas – radon in particular – are considered dangerous today but were offered as a treatment for rheumatism and gallstones in the past. Bathing in springs with warm sulfuric water, also not advised today, was said to relieve respiratory, digestive and skin ailments.

These days, wells at big pilgrimage destinations like Lourdes in France, or Walsingham in Norfolk, are still popular and attract many hoping for a miraculous cure. Smaller wells can also provide healing, of course, but I like to think of this as the soothing, spiritual kind of healing that a cool spring can provide, rather than more grandiose claims to cure serious complaints.

Watery Wisdom: Clooties

Approach many of the better-known holy wells, like Madron in Cornwall or St Boniface's Well in Munlochy, Inverness, and the first thing you see are hundreds of strips of cloth hanging from the overhanging tree branches. Each of these rags – known as clooties – represents one person's hopes for themselves or for another. The clootie is soaked in water from the well, rubbed on the injured part of the body, and then hung beside the well. The complaint is said to vanish as the cloth disintegrates. This is especially effective if carried out on a saint's day, or on the Celtic festivals of Imbolc (1 February), Beltane (1 May), Lughnasadh (1 August) or Samhain (1 November). It used to be thought that if anyone else removed the rag, they caught the illness of the person who placed it there, but this belief has perished with time, like the clooties themselves.

The practice of tying rags to trees beside healing wells is said to date back to pre-Christian times, although there is no hard evidence. It's had a resurgence recently, as more of us seek out sacred places, ancient customs and traditional ways, although these days it is often more about connecting with the past or making a wish than seeking healing.

Personally, I am among a growing band of folk who dislike clooties. Although they can lend a grotto-like, decorative quality to a well, to my mind they interfere with the essential spirit of the place. Mostly, they look untidy, especially if plastic ribbons or other items (teddy bears, artificial flowers or dolls, for example) are used instead of rags, which they all too frequently are. Not only is this unsightly, but also frequently non-biodegradable, littering the well and its surroundings for years. Trees are also damaged and bow beneath the weight of slowly disintegrating clutter. I would rather honour the place quietly by sitting beside the well, surrounded by the softness of nature, and leave nothing at all.

4. To Place A Curse

Visiting a well was not all about healing and prayer; some wells were visited with the express intention of doing harm. At these 'cursing wells', a mean-spirited visitor would scratch the name of a victim onto a stone. On payment of a fee, the custodian of the well would then cast the stone into the well. If the stone remained in the water, the curse – which generally involved pain, illness or even death inflicted on the unfortunate recipient – would be in effect. The victim could only remove the curse by paying the custodian a higher fee. One such cursing well was at St Elian's Church in Llanelian-yn-Rhos, Clwyd, where curses were placed until the nineteenth century, presumably making the custodian a tidy sum. Eventually, the vicar destroyed the well to put an end to what he regarded as superstitious nonsense.

5. To Incubate A Dream

As a well is a liminal place – a portal between the earthly realm and the 'other' world – it is an obvious location to tap into our own hidden depths, our subconscious, and to contact the spirit world. Historically, one way to do this was to access dreams by sleeping beside certain wells – a process known as 'dream incubation'.

These dreaming wells were said to emit radon, a colourless gas created by the radioactive decay of small amounts of uranium in rock and soil. Radon is considered dangerous to our health today, but in the past its power to induce sleep and encourage dreams was harnessed by those wanting to receive prophetic messages. Even today, incidences have been reported of people becoming unaccountably drowsy at the site of a holy well.

This could explain why certain wells, including St Madron and Sancreed in Cornwall, which emitted radon, became known as 'dream temples', with designated stone seats for pilgrims to spend the night. These were cold and uncomfortable beds but that was the point: disturbed sleep was necessary to prompt vivid and easily remembered dreams. In the seventeenth century, there are records of a disabled man called John Trelille washing in St Madron's Well before sleeping beside it. When he woke up, he reported that he was 'suddenly and perfectly cured'.

There is a precedent for dream incubation in Greek Asclepian temples of the Classical world, which were often located by a sacred spring. Those in need of healing would fast and participate in rituals intended to invoke a healing dream. And in Roman Britain, a dream temple dedicated to the Celtic god of healing, Nodens, was built at Lydney Park, in Gloucestershire, over several springs. It has a mosaic with an inscription referring to Victorinus the Interpreter, most likely the interpreter of dreams.

'When the well's dry, we know the worth of water.'
Benjamin Franklin, *Poor Richard's Almanac*

6. To Baptise A Child

One of my favourite weekend activities is to bundle my dog Fred into the back of the car and drive around the country looking for holy wells. My search, often accompanied by my friend and fellow well-enthusiast Cam, frequently takes me to ancient churches, especially those of St John the Baptist and St Ann. Both these saints are associated with water and with baptism especially, so it is no coincidence that their churches are near a water source, i.e. a spring. The early Christian Church built simple stone structures around springs, and these holy wells (as they became) were used for baptism. The Roman church replaced outdoor baptism with a font inside the building, but water was still drawn from the well and blessed by a priest before using. (The word 'font' derives from the Latin *fous*, which means fountain or spring.)

Baptism (or 'christening' as it has become known) is an important rite of the Christian Church and usually occurs early in a person's life. Early Christian baptism was naked, full immersion, which country folk believed also offered protection against illness, the Devil and witchcraft. Nuns and monks plunged naked into cold water, sometimes breaking ice to do so, to be in a state of innocence before their Creator.

The purpose of baptism is to wash away original sin (the evil supposedly innate in all human beings), permit entry into the kingdom of heaven and welcome someone into the Church. These days it is more likely to be performed by affusion – pouring water over the head above a font – rather than total submersion. (Unless you are a member of the Baptist Church, which puts full-body immersion at the centre of its beliefs.)

The use of consecrated water to purify, wash away sins, spiritually cleanse and be 'born again' is common to many religions and faiths globally, from Ancient Egyptian rituals, to Shinto, Confucian and Hindu customs, such as bathing in the Ganges. It is still much practised, from Christian christenings (and the simple act of dipping a hand into a basin on entry into a church) to the large-scale Hindu festival of Kumbh Mela in India, where pilgrims immerse themselves at the confluence of two rivers.

'He poureth water into a bason,
and began to wash the disciples' feet.'
John 13:4-5, The Bible

Watery Wisdom: a puzzling stone basin

Bullaun stones are mysterious Irish stones that have a man-made hollow at their centre to collect rainwater. There are various theories about their original purpose, including use as a baptismal font or a holy blessing well. Alternatively, they may have been intended to grind corn or crush herbs. Small round stones incised with crosses were also placed in them to be used as prayer stones: pilgrims turned them in a clockwise direction while praying. The water that collected in the basin was believed to have curative properties, as was water found in 'cupmarks' – miniature wells found naturally in rocks.

How to Dowse

Locating a source of clean freshwater has always been a vital skill for survival. When it is not apparent, i.e. no spring can be found, a method known as dowsing can be used to find underground water. When it has been located, a shaft can then be drilled down to reach it, creating a well.

Tools used for dowsing include a Y-shaped hazel branch, L-shaped metal rods and pendulums. The dowser walks slowly with their tool of choice held loosely in their hands (or hand, in case of the pendulum). Using observation and, sometimes, intuition, they look out for signs such as a swing to the right or left, or the rods crossing over; with the hazel branch, a twitch; and with a pendulum, a rotational swing.

In his book *How to Read Water*, Tristan Gooley points out that as the water table – an underground reservoir that rises and falls with rainfall (see below) – is found everywhere, water can be found anywhere if you drill deep enough. Dowsing reveals the depth rather than the existence of water. Rivers can give a clue as to how deep to go, as they have a base level they rarely drop below, which indicates the height of the water table surrounding it.

Watery Wisdom: Where Wells Begin – Aquifers

It helps to understand the miracle of wells if you know where they come from. When rainwater seeps through the soil, it saturates porous rock or sediment lying beneath the water table. This is known as an aquifer. Water can move through the aquifer, intersecting with the surface as springs and wetlands, or at man-made interventions – wells. Much of our drinking water comes from aquifers, although they have become depleted and contaminated, like much of our freshwater, through agricultural and industrial practices.

Myths and Legends of Wells

The value of wells as sources of life-giving water, combined with their magical appearance from deep underground, mean that they were highly valued in ancient times. Consequently, no end of myths and legends sprang up around them: some were linked to their healing properties, while others to their associations with fertility and the goddess, or to the world of fairies and piskies.

Mystical women of the well

According to Janet Bord in her book *Cures and Curses: ritual and cult at holy wells*, wells and springs were seen as entrances into the body and womb of Mother Earth. As mentioned previously, there was also a belief in the procreative power of water, which was seen as the source of fertility. Certain goddesses were, therefore, assigned to these holy wells – a practice taken up during the advent of Christianity, when earlier pagan sites were rededicated to its own saints.

Many wells have been attributed to St Ann, the grandmother of Jesus, and churches dedicated to her are often good indicators that there is a well nearby. The pagan precedent of St Ann is the Celtic mother-goddess of springs, rivers and wisdom, variously named as Danu, Annis, Anu, Modron or Matrona.

St Brigid, formerly the Celtic goddess Brighde, who we have already met on page 6, is still honoured in Ireland with pilgrimages to wells dedicated to her that take place on Imbolc (1 February), also known as St Brigid's Day. The most significant is to the well at Faughart, in County Louth, believed to be her birthplace. The Brigid's Way Pilgrimage starts there and ends nine days later at Brigid's Well, in Kildare.

Ladywell in Lewisham, south London, was once the site of a spring known as Our Lady's Well, which was a stop-off point for pilgrims on their way to Canterbury. It is now buried beneath residential housing, but its name reminds us that many wells were rededicated to the Virgin Mary, having once been the haunts of pagan goddesses and priestesses.

The Romans similarly re-appropriated native well deities to honour their own goddesses. One such was Coventina, a Romano-British goddess of wells and springs who presided over a well at Carrawburgh, on Hadrian's Wall. Now hidden beneath a marshy swamp, the site is marked by a standing stone. When excavated, a relief of three water nymphs was found in the well, alongside many coins, votive objects and slabs dedicated to Coventina.

Fabulous creatures who live in a well

It is an indication of the value once placed on wells that various terrifying animals and monsters were said to guard them. Chief among these is the watery brigade: eels, serpents and monster fish, although phantom dogs have also been spotted hanging around well-heads at dusk. These unfriendly spirits had to be kept sweet with offerings, otherwise disasters and epidemics would strike the local community. Legendary dragons also lurked within the depths of wells, getting larger, more furious and increasingly dangerous, until they were slain by a hero.

One such dragon lived in the Dragon's Well, Brinsop, in Herefordshire, until it was vanquished by St George, an event recorded on the tympanum of the nearby church of St George. (A plaque in the churchyard now marks the location of the well.) The most famous, however, is the Lambton Worm, which emerged from a well to kill livestock, steal children and generally rampage. He was eventually killed by John Lambton, who had thrown the Worm down the well in the first place when it was young and tiny. This series of events was immortalised in a song where the story of 'the queer worm i' the well' that 'growed an aaful size' is told in Northumberland dialect.

Where the fairy folk dwell

Sit quietly beside certain wells and springs at dusk, and you may see ethereal beings dancing, feasting and making merry in the fading light. It is said that those places where the water flows from the earth are natural spots for fairies to appear, emerging through a portal to scamper about on the terrestrial plane.

Wales has several fairy wells to test this theory, including the Virtuous Well in Trellech (see page 2), the Fairy Well near Abergavenny (both in Monmouthshire) and the Fairy Well at Laugharne, in Carmarthenshire. Tempting though it may be to introduce yourself and join the fairy folk, this would be foolish: there is a danger that you will be lured into Fairyland and not return. Or you may find yourself in Fairyland, like a shepherd boy on the Preseli Hills in Wales did, and like it too much. He spoilt his personal paradise, however, by disobeying fairy rules and drinking from a fountain where the golden fishes swam. Immediately and without ceremony, he was deposited back on the hillside with his very non-sprite-like sheep.

In Devon and Cornwall, you may encounter a piskie (pixie) guarding the well. Piskies are like fairies but more rough and ready: they are often naked and mischievous, and roam about in the wilder places. Notable among these haunts is the Piskies' Well in Pelynt, Cornwall, an atmospheric stone well-house covered with moss and liverworts. Over the years, many pins have been dropped into its stone basin and many tea lights lit to placate the grumpy piskie who guards it. Visitors would be wise to enter respectfully, otherwise bad luck will come their way. Treat the well with reverence, however, and fortune and good health will be bestowed upon you.

Trees and wells: perfect companions

The magic of visiting a well is often amplified by a tree-lined path that leads towards it. The sheltering boughs of this sylvan tunnel draw you on towards your destination, and when you reach it, you may find more trees standing above it like guardians. Here are the trees you are most likely to find:

Hawthorn, a most magical tree, is regarded as a threshold to the Otherworld. Its tangle of thorny branches is often draped with clootie rags (see page 10).

Spot an **alder** and the chances are that there is water nearby – they grow well in damp conditions and won't rot in water (Venice is built on alder stakes). A branch of the alder also makes a good dowsing rod, as do branches of hazel.

In Irish mythology, the Well of Segais (also known as the Well of Connla) surfaces in a grove of nine **hazel** trees and is home to the salmon of wisdom.

Yew is also commonly seen near wells: a couple of ancient yews grow over the Chalice Well in Glastonbury.

Watery Wisdom: Fairy Folk

The Middle English word 'fairy' derives from the French *fae*. It was thought that calling fairies directly by that word risked offending them, so they were referred to as 'good people' or 'fair folk'. In Wales, the fairy folk are known as *Y twlwyth teg* (the fair folk) or *Ellyllon* (shining beings), a reference to their blonde hair and shimmering presence.

Ten UK Wells to Visit

There are many, many more wells than I have listed here but space prevents naming them all. These are some of my favourites. Hunt more out on OS maps (look for a blue W or SPR) or on helpful websites like www.insearchofholywellsandhealingsprings.com, as many aren't recorded.

1. St Winefride's Well, Holywell, Flintshire

Known as one of the Seven Wonders of Wales, this is no hole in the ground but a sizeable well with a large pool for total immersion, a chapel, a museum and gatehouse. It is, in fact, a well complex that still attracts thousands of pilgrims every year, most hoping for a cure to an illness or affliction. Evidence of past miracles – abandoned crutches that were no longer needed, and so on – hangs from the walls. The well was founded in the seventh century around the legend of St Winefride: she was a virgin pursued by Caradoc, a prince's son, who attempted to rape her. She fled to the church for safety but he, in retaliation for being spurned, beheaded her and a spring rose where her head fell. Fortunately, her head was placed back on her body by her uncle St Beuno. Winefride went on to become a nun and after her death, a cult grew up centred upon her relics. Pilgrims still kneel to pray on St Beuno's stone, which is in the bathing pool and has red stains, believed to be traces of Winefride's blood. There is also a shrine to the saint where offerings and rosaries are left in prayer and gratitude.

2. Madron Well, Madron, West Penwith, Cornwall

The path through tangled woodland, marsh and briar to this famous healing well is as magical as the destination. Many weary feet have walked along it, drawn by the circular well's healing reputation. Clootie rags hanging from trees all around are evidence of these visits. Madron was either the patron saint of healing and cures, a priest from Brittany, or possibly a Christianisation of Modron, depending on which account you read. Modron, which means 'Mother' in Old Celtic, was the mother of the virgin, and represents the earth mother and the dark or waning moon.

3. Chalice Well and the White Spring, Glastonbury, Somerset

Glastonbury has been a pilgrimage destination for centuries and has always been regarded as a place of healing and transformation. It has two important, yet very different, water sources. Water from the White Spring gushes from the foot of the Tor, sparkling with calcite into a candlelit temple, converted from a Victorian pumping station. A series of pools and shrines create a numinous atmosphere. Water from the Chalice Well, on the other hand, is coloured red from iron deposits (it is also known as the Blood Spring) and emerges into sunlit gardens, designated World Peace Garden; it is also where Joseph of Arimathea is said to have buried the Holy Grail.

4. St Ann's Well, Great Malvern, Worcestershire

Growing up in Malvern, I often walked up the ninety-nine steps from town, then followed a zig-zag path to this well. The side of the Hills overlooking the town and the plain beyond was a welcome place to pause, draw breath from the climb, sit and take in the view. The water splashing into a scallop-shaped bowl from the mouth of a marble dolphin was an especially welcome sight after the steep climb. Built in the early nineteenth century, the well house and pump rooms (which included hot and cold baths) were a popular destination for Victorians taking the water cure (see page 73). The water was valued for its purity: it contains no minerals in solution. These days, walkers can also be refreshed at the café, with its selection of cakes and tea.

5. The Wizard's Well, Alderley Edge, Cheshire

Alderley Edge, a wooded sandstone escarpment that overlooks the Cheshire Plain, is a land wreathed with myths and mysteries. One of the most arresting of these is the Wizard's Well, found a little way beyond the National Trust's walking routes. The water that drips into a small stone trough from the rock is said to have healing properties, but it also has magical associations. Above it is the moss-covered bearded head of a wizard, and beneath him, crudely carved into the rock, is this couplet:

'Drink of this and take thy fill
For the water falls by the wizhard's will.'

Both are said to be the work of local stonemason Robert Garner in the mid-nineteenth century, who was inspired by the legend of the Wizard of the Edge. This tells of a wizard (Merlin) who buys a farmer's horse to complete his underground army (King Arthur's sleeping knights), waiting in slumber beneath the Edge until they are awakened to save Albion in its hour of need. Robert Garner's descendant, Alan Garner, was inspired by the legend when he wrote the spellbinding children's fantasy novel *The Weirdstone of Brisingamen*.

6. St Margaret's Well, Binsey, Oxford

During the Middle Ages, pilgrims flocked to this 'treacle well', drawn by claims that its waters offered cures for all ills. ('Treacle' derives from an older word 'triacle', meaning a medicinal balm or salve.) These amazing curative powers are said to have been summoned by St Frideswide, Oxford's patron saint, who caused water to bubble up from the earth after she had escaped to this quiet spot when pursued by Algar, a Mercian king, intent to make her his wife. Algar tracked her down and was about to claim her, when he was struck blind. Frideswide, showing great compassion and forgiveness, struck the well and restored his sight. The notion of a 'treacle well' appealed to local resident Lewis Carroll, who mentioned it in *Alice in Wonderland*: three little sisters lived at the bottom of one, sustained only by treacle.

7. Mother Shipton's Dropping (Petrifying) Well, Knaresborough, North Yorkshire

Despite becoming a major tourist destination, the Dropping Well still feels mysterious and otherworldly. This is largely due to the fantastical shapes made by water 'dropping' over a sharp ledge and 'petrifying' anything that gets in its way under layers of mineral deposits. Further magic is added by the story of the famous prophetess Mother Shipton. Legend has it that she was born in 1488 in a cave near the well during a thunderstorm, when there was sulphur in the air and cracks in the ground. Her powers were used to curse her enemies and to foretell the future (she predicted the Great Fire of London, among other historical moments); the accuracy of these predictions grew her notoriety.

8. St Issui's Well, Patrishow, Powys

I found this well as we drove up a country lane to visit the Norman church of St Issui in Patrishow, a village in Wales. Issui was a hermit who was murdered by a passing stranger and subsequently canonised. The church is remote, secluded, ancient and well worth a visit to see the fresco of the skeleton on its wall. The well was an additional and delightful discovery. It surfaces in a small stone building beside the road and a small stream on the approach to the church; you clamber down a little to reach it. Water from the well is said to heal eye complaints and my short-sighted partner bathed his eyes in it hopefully, reporting that it was 'soothing at least' – as is the well itself: a more tranquil and magical spot is hard to find.

9. St Boniface's Well, Munlochy, Inverness

This Scottish well is famous for the clootie offerings (see page 10) that swamp it and festoon the footpath leading towards it. These include underwear, shoes, soft toys and too many miscellaneous items to mention here. Many are put there in thanks for healing, while others are prayers and wishes for healing or luck to come. However well intentioned, they are an example of how such offerings can become unsightly and affect the natural world that surrounds the well.

10. The Seven Wells, Bisley, Gloucestershire

This handsome stone structure, built in 1863, is notable for two things. Firstly, the copious amount of water that gushes from spouts beneath five Gothic arches and two side springs into a pond and stone troughs. Secondly, the annual well blessing ceremony which has taken place on Ascension Day for over fifty years. Following a church service, school children bring floral creations to decorate the well while a band plays a hymn.

Watery Wellness: A Water Ceremony Around a Well

This is how Kate Smart of Malvern Dowsers (see page 2) honoured the well and the goddess of the well in my house. It is a simple ceremony, which can be repeated at any well or water source to show respect and reverence for a water source, and to help heal any that have been neglected or polluted. The words of the ceremony are Kate's.

Place symbolic offerings on or near the well.

Kate brought flowers from her garden, water from her well, an abalone shell and a porcelain whale to represent the sea, some coral beads, and a light-blue candle. She arranged these in a mandala shape and lit the candle.

Everyone gathers in a circle around the well.

We were invited to be comfortable and close our eyes. Each person brought a gift or offering for the well. These were held close to our hearts as we took three deep, slow breaths. There was a pause.

Someone says this:

The purpose of this ceremony is to
bless and protect this sacred well
and allow for flow and abundance.

We are here as healers, friends
and fellow inhabitants of this land.

May peace abide in this place and throughout our lives,
allowing the flow of water to cleanse,
heal and refresh us and the land.

Goddess of this well, we honour you and your home
and make an offering to acknowledge your
special place here long before us.

I call to the spirits and nature beings to bless
and protect your home and allow us to dwell
in harmony with you.

I will be quiet now and listen for your voice.

Everyone stands silently and listens, then takes three deep, slow breaths and opens their eyes. Each person places their gift on the well.

Someone says:

Thank you for speaking to us,
goddess of the well.
Please accept our gifts.

A Simple Well Ritual

A favourite church of mine is St John the Baptist in the village of Hope Bagot, near Ludlow, in Shropshire. It was built above a spring and beside a very old yew tree – dated as more than 1,600 years old – which makes this a very likely place of pre-Christian worship.

The first time I visited, the venerable old tree had suffered a mighty blow during a storm that caused a large bough to crash to the ground, covering the well with splintered bark and dark green leaves. The only way I could experience the well was to listen to the sound of the water trickling from the bank.

After hearing that some of the fallen tree had been removed, I returned with a friend, Cam. The well, with its stone surround, was clearly visible, although it was still cluttered with branches and leaves. We both stood and looked at it, and I wondered how best to honour this special place. As I dithered and pondered, Cam knelt and, still wearing her knitted gloves, cleared the debris away. Water rushed into the cleared space, full of energy and vitality. It was exactly the right thing to do.

Knowing how to behave at a sacred space such as a holy well is an important part of any visit. Here are some simple rituals to deepen the experience.

Sit quietly beside it, listening to any sounds – the rustle of a bush, the trill of a bird, the wind in the trees – and tune into the spirit of the place. This would be a good time to meditate, set an intention or think about any healing you want help with.

Take a sample. The boot of my car always has a few clean, glass jars ready to fill with water gathered from special watery places. These jars are labelled and stored on a bookshelf and are a reminder of where I have been and what I experienced there. The water can also be charged in the light of a full moon and used in rituals. I think of them as my library of sacred waters.

Before taking a sample, I always ask the water source for permission, and thank it afterwards for its generosity. Remember to label the jar with the name of the place and the date. If you plan to visit another well on the same day or at some time in the future, take an additional sample in a different jar, carry it with you and spill the contents into the next well. This makes a lovely spiritual connection between the two places and bookends your journey. As you tip the water into the second place, set an intention or make a prayer, then thank both wells.

The act of transporting holy water has an historical precedent. Ampullae containing water brought by pilgrims from Walsingham, in Norfolk, have been found buried at the edges of fields in the Midlands. It is thought that they were intended to encourage a good harvest.

Leave an offering. This is a good way to establish a connection with the well, as long as you are mindful of what you leave. Evidence of offerings left in water has been found dating as far back as the Mesolithic period, and the practice has continued into modern times with 'clootie' rags being tied to trees around wells (see page 10) in exchange for healing or an answer to a prayer. Biodegradable, natural offerings such as a flower, a leaf or a piece of bark fallen from a tree are best. You could float petals or a flower on the water as you speak your intention or hopes, or write the words on the back of a leaf or piece of bark and slip it into the water and watch it float away.

Chapter Two

Still Waters

Lakes, pools and natural swimming ponds

'If there is magic on this planet, it is contained in water.'

Loren Eiseley, American anthropologist, philosopher and nature writer

Whereas rivers ceaselessly rush and flow, lakes and pools are calm and serene. Apart from the wind troubling the surface of the water or the splash of a bird coming into land, lakes are still and mirror-like, reflecting the sky and the passing movement of the clouds. They are contained, surrounded by land – often high mountains – atmospheric and unfathomable.

We tend to think of lakes as natural places that have always existed. While this is true of those formed by the movement of glaciers, fed by mountain springs or an underground source, many others are man-made, such as reservoirs, quarry lakes and those dug out for recreational purposes, such as boating lakes in parks and fishing ponds.

However they were created, these large bodies of water always draw us to them, whether it is to swim, fish, paddle or simply sit beside and watch the patterns and colours on their surface.

Unlike rivers, which grow over time as they travel through the land, excavating as they go, lakes are static and will eventually vanish, filled in with plants, sediment and mud. Many are rumoured to be 'bottomless', forbidding places of dread; others are only reached by a long walk into the heart of remote, wild mountains. These enigmatic qualities account for the many legends and stories that surround them, most involving creatures who lurk in their depths, or fairy folk who have made the underwater world their kingdom and the glass-like surface a portal to enter it.

Intrigued by one such legend, I headed for Llyn y Fan Fach in Bannau Brycheiniog (Brecon Beacons) in Wales. This is the haunt of the Lady of the Lake: a beautiful girl – said to be a fairy princess – who emerged from her watery kingdom beneath the lake one day and met a young farmer on the shore. He was suitably beguiled by her loveliness and asked her three times to marry him, presenting her with a loaf of bread each time. The first couple of times she replied, 'Unbaked is thy bread/I will not have thee,' but on the third, for some unaccountable reason, she agreed, stipulating that she would leave him if he hit her three times: 'Strike me without cause three times/And you shall lose me.'

She brought a dowry of magical animals to the marriage and many happy years followed spent at his farm near the village of Myddfai, where they raised two sons. Then the inevitable happened: he hit her three times. Unsurprisingly, she fled back to the lake with her animals, only resurfacing on occasion to teach her sons the art of herbal medicine. They went on to become physicians to the English royal court, known as the Physicians of Myddfai, and she is still rumoured to appear at Lughnasadh around 1 August. There is no account of what became of the farmer.

I thought about this tale as I walked the gravel path up the steep hill to Llyn y Fan Fach.

The lake wasn't in sight yet but the mighty range of the Black Mountains – peaking with Fan Brycheiniog – was, its corrugated, sculptural forms deepened by shadows from the bright summer sun. The Afon Sawdde (River Sawdde) ran alongside the path, breaking over rocks to create little waterfalls and pools. Swallows swooped low overhead and, high in the sky, a red kite circled.

The serenity of the moment, however, was disturbed by several earth-moving vehicles employed by Welsh Water, which rattled past with irritating frequency, trailing clouds of dust as they went. The lake is dammed (the work was completed in 1919) and construction work was going on, presumably to repair or maintain it. As I stepped aside to let another gravel-laden truck thunder past, I remembered that the water that came out of the taps in my house in Herefordshire was from a reservoir in Wales (the people of Llanelli benefit from the one at Llyn y Fach Fan). I was also aware that several Welsh valleys were dammed and flooded in the 1960s, and entire communities evacuated, to provide water for the Midlands, Cheshire and Liverpool. The drowning of the village of Capel Celyn in 1965 to create the Tryweryn reservoir, in particular, provoked Welsh anger at the destruction of Welsh-language communities and culture, and the slogan: '*Cofiwch Dryweryn*' ('Remember Tryweryn') became a nationalist rallying cry.

Fortunately, by the time I approached the lake, it was lunchtime and the construction traffic stopped. As the workers headed for Portakabins and mugs of tea, I crested a hillock. Llyn y Fan Fach was revealed. It was indeed the perfect home for a Lady of the Lake.

The lake was formed during the last Ice Age by a glacier carving a steep-sided, amphitheatre-shaped cwm out of the sandstone. This was evident in the escarpment, Bannau Sir Gaer, which towered above the lake, all crinkled ridges and forbidding shadows. The lake lay placidly beneath it, a deep-green pool glittering with captured sunlight. I scrambled down to the water's edge over angular chunks of rock and spongey mud. The water level was low, due to a recent period of drought, but the lake remained expansive and still, only ruffled by a cooling breeze.

Llyn y Fan Fach is not an enormous lake (its name means 'little lake by the peak' – a larger lake, Llyn y Fan Fawr or 'big lake by the peak', is two miles further east) so, obeying the rules of pilgrimage where circumambulation is preferred to a direct approach, I set off to walk around it. Walking anywhere, the simple act of putting one foot in front of the other, steadies the mind, and walking around the lake felt especially calming. There were the ever-changing patterns of the water to watch, the sounds of the red kites whistling to each other overhead to hear, and the welcoming breeze to feel on my hot neck. On the high ridge above, tiny silhouettes of other walkers were outlined against the sun. A footpath from the lake takes you up to this point, which has seemingly never-ending views of the surrounding landscape. My path, however, was obstructed halfway round the lake by construction work at the dam, so I was reluctantly forced to retrace my steps following a semi-circular route back to where I had started, before beginning the descent.

As I walked down the hill, I puzzled over how the dam and the construction workers had played such a prominent part in my walk to the lake, when I had been propelled there by tales of a fairy princess and an underwater world. Back home, I did a bit more research. I discovered that the dam had largely been built by 200 conscientious objectors during the First World War. They had been released from prison – where they were incarcerated as punishment for refusing to fight – to do this hard, manual labour. Mostly from north-west England and the Midlands, they had replaced the original workforce who had refused to work in such a remote and challenging place. Who were these men, I wondered, far from home, prepared to become society's outcasts and undergo this harsh punishment for a crime of conscience? Their story is a modern legend of sorts, and they are its heroes. Now I think of the lake as haunted as much by their ghosts as that of the spectral Lady of the Lake.

The Lady of the Lake

The most famous Lady of the Lake is she of Arthurian legend. However, rather than relate to one individual, 'Lady of the Lake' is a title given to many and various ethereal aquatic sorceresses, depending on which account you read. In *Le Morte d'Arthur*, Thomas Malory's fifteenth-century tale, she surfaces from the lake to give King Arthur, who is accompanied by the wizard Merlin, the sword Excalibur.

A second Lady of the Lake, according to Malory, is Nimue, also known as Morgan Le Fey, who appears in various accounts of the legend as a demi-goddess, necromancer, healer and fairy woman. She invariably has an evil role to play, usually plotting Arthur's downfall (although, confusingly, she was also one of four women in black who ferried his body across the river to the Isle of Avalon, where she used her magic to save his life). Morgan Le Fey is related to mermaids of the Breton coast called Morganes, Mari Morgan or Morgan, who enchanted sailors, in a similar fashion to a siren (see page 114), and either lured them underwater to paradise or drowned them.

In Welsh folklore, ladies of the lake are known as Gwragedd Annwn, the women of the Annwn (Underworld or Summerland). They lived at the bottom of lonely lakes (usually in the mountains, e.g. Llyn Barfog, Llyn Crymlyn, Llyn Cau and Llyn y Fan Fach) in castles with beautiful gardens, and wore blue, white or green robes. They were prone to seducing male lovers by trickery and then cruelly abandoning them; they are sometimes spotted in the twilight on a summer's evening, dressed in green and accompanied by their white dogs, as their milk-white cows graze on the lake shore. Legend has it that a greedy farmer stole one of these cows from the shore of Lake Cau. The cow became well-known for its rich and plentiful milk and healthy calves. When it was old and non-productive, the farmer took it to be slaughtered but, as the slaughterman raised his knife, a loud cry sounded from the lake. A fairy woman dressed in customary green robes summoned the cow and all its offspring and took them back beneath the surface of the lake to safety.

Three Other Lake Ladies

Ceridwen. This enchantress of Welsh medieval legend lived near Llyn Tegid (Bala Lake) in north Wales. She is seen by modern pagans as the Celtic goddess of rebirth, transformation and inspiration because of her cauldron, which has poetic and transformative powers.

Melusine. A female European spirit of fresh water who appears with her two sisters at a fountain in the middle of a forest. She is usually depicted as having a serpent or fish bottom half, much like a mermaid. Her legends relate to France, Luxembourg and the Low Countries.

Li Ban. The story of the Irish mermaid Li Ban, dates from the sixth century (see page 113). She was the beautiful daughter of Eochaidh, King of Ireland, and, along with her dog, was the only survivor when her father's palace and lands were flooded by water from a magic well. The flooded land became Lough Neagh.

Living alone and miserably in a bower under the lough, Li Ban prayed to the river god Danu to be turned into a salmon, so she could swim with the fish for company. Danu, mean-spiritedly, half-granted her wish and turned her into a mermaid and her dog into an otter. They swam out of the lough and into the sea, where they drifted for the next 300 years, until she was caught in fishing nets by a monk. Once ashore, she was baptised and then died having been promised a heavenly reward. She has since been known as the Mermaid Saint and is celebrated on her feast day, on 27 January.

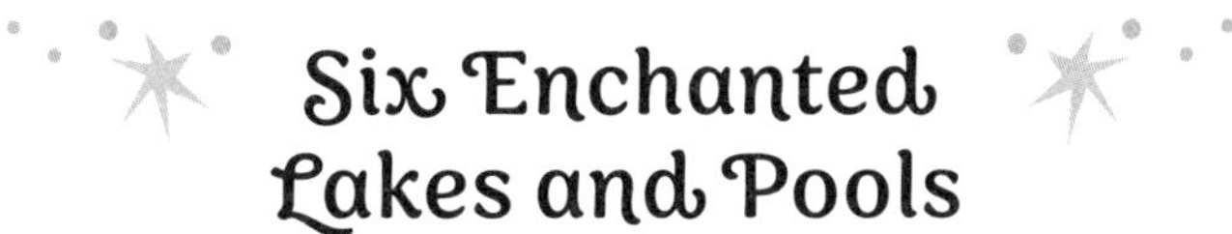

Six Enchanted Lakes and Pools

1. A LADY, A SCOUNDREL AND A STORM WOMAN: Dozmary Pool, Bodmin Moor, Cornwall

High on Bodmin Moor, alone and silently reflecting the sky above, the bowl of Dozmary Pool is shrouded in early-morning mist and myth in equal measure. One legend recounts how a knight of the Round Table, Sir Bedivere, returned the mighty sword Excalibur here after King Arthur was mortally wounded at the Battle of Camlann.

It certainly looks like the sort of place the Lady of the Lake would inhabit and it is easy to imagine her slender white arm surfacing from its depths to clutch the sword, before taking it down into the inky deep. In actuality, the association between the lake and King Arthur was created by the poet Tennyson and monetised by a local landowner who, for a fee, took Arthurian tourists out onto the water in a boat to look for the Lady.

A more potent and local legend is that of Jan Tregeagle – a seventeenth-century magistrate of ill repute – who made a pact with the Devil. In return for a life of power and riches, his part of the bargain, claimed on his death by his satanic master, was to repeat impossible tasks for eternity. One was to empty the bottomless[1] pool using only a limpet shell with a hole in it. It is said that his desperate wails as he continues with this thankless task are still carried by the wind across the moor. This wind, like all of those on Bodmin Moor, is said to originate from the clawed hands of the Old Storm Woman who lives in the pool, stirring up the water, and creating winds as she does so.

2. A WISHING TREE, A HEALING WELL AND A BRUTAL CURE: Loch Maree, Wester Ross, Scotland

The magic of Loch Maree is largely due to its number of islands: sixty-six altogether, some of which have the remains of ancient Caledonian pinewood. It is a wonderful place to kayak, camp and even swim (though midges can be a nuisance). One of the largest islands, Isle Maree, has a ruined chapel, which is believed to be the eighth-century hermitage of St Mael Ruba (who died in 722). It also has an oak tree, once visited by Queen Victoria, studded with coins from those seeking answers to their prayers, and a holy well credited with healing powers. One brutal cure was to tie the sick or insane person to a boat with a horsehair rope and then tow them around the island several times, before immersing them in the well. The loch is also credited with its own monster, called Muc-sheilch, which loosely translates as 'turtle-pig'.

3. A MALEVOLENT MERMAID: Doxey's Pool, The Roaches, Staffordshire

Single men should be wary when passing this tiny pool on the Staffordshire/Derbyshire border – a beautiful woman may appear and sing to them, luring them towards her, taking them deeper and deeper into the water. When they reach the deepest part of the pool, she will reveal her true self: a green, buck-toothed creature, half-woman, half-fish, who then drags them to their watery doom.

This is the legendary Jenny Greenteeth (see page 57): a malevolent spirit often found inhabiting the grim waters of isolated pools and rivers. She does not just appear to men, however. In 1949, Miss Florence Pettit

---

1 The notion that the pool is bottomless was disproved in 1866, 1869 and 1876, when drought caused water levels to drop dramatically. These days it is estimated to be around 3 metres deep.

claims she saw a weird creature resembling Jenny Greenteeth emerge from Doxey's Pool just before she took her morning swim.

This is not the only pool in the Peak District troubled by a malignant spirit: nearby Blakemere Pool (said to be linked to Doxey's Pool by a deep subterranean passage) is rumoured to be haunted by an aquatic ghost, and Mermaid Pool near Kinder Scout has a mermaid who, tantalisingly, only appears on Easter Sunday.

Located 1,600 ft (488 m) above sea level on the gritstone escarpment The Roaches, Doxey's Pool is said never to run dry and, like other mysterious bodies of water, be bottomless. It certainly has a haunting atmosphere and is a place of pilgrimage for some – an altar and the remains of offerings are often seen on the pool's shore.

4. A BOUNDARY BETWEEN TWO WORLDS: Llyn Fawr, Blaenrhondda, South Glamorgan

Evidence that this lake was once considered sacred was found when it was drained during the process of turning it into a reservoir in the twentieth century. A remarkable hoard of twenty-one tools and weapons was revealed, including a big bronze cauldron, thought to be thrown into the lake as offerings by Bronze and Iron Age people. The reflective waters of the lake, which is located on the northern flanks of Craig-y-Llyn mountain, were seen as a boundary between two worlds – this world and the Celtic underworld, Annwn. Offerings dispatched into its waters were gifts to the gods in return for good harvests, mild winters and success in battle. A green lady also frequents the lake, appearing once every seven years, making necklaces from rowan berries that turn miraculously into gold.

5. A SACRED SPRING: Loch Sheanta, Flodigarry, Isle of Skye, Scotland

Now hidden, appropriately, in a hazel copse, this sacred spring at the western end of Loch Sheanta was traditionally used for healing. Invalids would circle the spring three times *deosil* (sunwise or clockwise) before drinking the water. Many tied rags to nearby trees or left offerings of pins and coins. The spring drains into the loch, once full of trout left untroubled and unfished because taking any would 'signal judgements to follow upon it'. Similarly, it was considered unlucky, and foolish, to cut down the trees that surround the spring, which it was believed were the homes of nature spirits. The loch itself lies near the foothills of the mighty Quiraing mountains, a landscape of strange and monumental rock formations worthy of the books of J. R. R. Tolkien.

6. HEALING WATERS: Loch mo-Naire, Strathnaver, Scotland

This dark and moody loch surrounded by distant forbidding hills was a pilgrimage destination for the sick until the mid-nineteenth century. The cure was to go down to the shore at midnight, take a sip of the loch's water and then remove all clothes before walking backwards into the loch. There pilgrims would immerse themselves three times before making offerings of silver coins (some of these are in the Strathnaver Museum in Thurso, a fascinating place with many interesting objects related to the area's mystical past). This cure was said to be especially powerful on the first Monday in August, and increasingly so if the day fell on 4 August. This may have some association with the Celtic festival of Lughnasadh – held to mark the harvest season – celebrated on 1 August.

The mystical power of the loch is credited to a legend about a local witch who had in her possession magic crystal stones that, when placed water, gave it the power to cure all 'the ills to which flesh is her'. A member of the clan Gordon tried to steal them from her but rather than give them up, she threw them into the loch, declaring that from then on anyone – unless their surname was Gordon – would be healed by drinking or bathing in its waters.

Folkloric Creatures of the Lakes

A still stretch of water has magic about it. It is easy to understand how lakes, like wells, were thought to be portals to another world, especially on a cold winter morning when a shrouding mist hangs above the water, or on a bright summer's day when the heavenly blue sky is reflected mirror-like on the surface. Many mythical creatures were thought to dwell in the shadowy depths of lakes and pools, or to emerge ghost-like through the mist. Among this aquatic pantheon are water maidens, shapeshifting horses and bulls, monsters, and even faery cows.

Water horses

An encounter with a water horse is best avoided. Some are half-beast, half-human, others shapeshift to become handsome young men or women. Few have good intentions. In Scotland, most lochs have their own legends of dangerous young horses called kelpies. On a good day, kelpies play relatively harmless pranks, but on a bad day they wreak havoc, sinking ships, drowning men, conjuring up storms, even eating animals and humans. Although they look like and associate with normal horses, if you touch them, or attempt to ride them, they will drag you under. Also, unlike normal horses, they might smack the water three times with their tails, making a thunderous sound, before vanishing in a flash of lightning.

One kelpie legend concerns a man called McGregor who, weary from walking, stopped by Loch Slochd and wished aloud for a horse. Incredibly, a horse with a saddle and bridle appeared, so he mounted it. The horse was not a horse, however, but a kelpie. It did not obey the man's commands and instead galloped off towards the lake. Terrified, McGregor prayed fervently and was thrown off. The kelpie kept going into the water, but McGregor managed to hold on to the bridle, dislodged it and took it home. He unwittingly found the kelpie's weak spot: anyone who gets hold of a kelpie's bridle can use it for benevolent magic, as can their family and descendants.

Tizzie Whizzies

These mini-monsters with a hedgehog's body, a squirrel's tail, and bee-like wings and antennae are said to roam the shores of Lake Windermere in Cumbria, squeaking crazily as they go. They were first spotted in 1900 by a boatman offering trips to tourists, which led many to believe that he had invented them to increase his trade. You may also come across Bownessie, a monster akin to the one in Loch Ness, in Lake Windermere, and elves and fairies who have made Elva Hill on the banks of Bassenthwaite Lake their home and an entrance to the Otherworld.

Water monsters

The most famous of these is, of course, Nessie, the humpbacked creature of Loch Ness in the Scottish Highlands. Various sightings describe seeing a fish- or whale-like beast or a dragon in the water, although several have been proved to be hoaxes. Oral tales of water monsters in the loch have been told for generations and may have kickstarted the search for an actual creature. Legend has it that St Columba, seeing a friend threatened by Nessie, raised his hand when the monster appeared, then made the sign of the cross, which allowed his friend to swim safely to the opposite bank.

Other lochs in Scotland have their fair share of monsters, as do lakes in Wales. Llyn Tegid (Bala Lake) in Gwynedd – the biggest natural lake in the country – boasts a monster called Teggie. In other lakes (Llyn Llion and Llyn Barfog near Brynberian bridge, and Llyn yr Afanc near Betws y Coed), the Afanc, who resembles a crocodile, beaver or platypus, depending on the source, dwells and surfaces occasionally to cause havoc, drag the unsuspecting to their doom and create floods. It is told that King Arthur, who regularly appears in legends of lakes, dragged the Afanc from Llyn Barfog, a remote lake in the hills above Aberdovey. The locals had been troubled by the monster killing livestock and causing havoc until Arthur stepped in and pulled it from the lake with magical chains. He then either killed it or dragged it to Llyn Cau, depending on which version you read. A stone beside a footpath at Llyn Cau, known as Carn March Arthur (the Stone of Arthur's Horse's Hoof), is imprinted with a hoof print said to have been made by King Arthur's horse as he battled with the creature.

Lake Swimming

Much has been made of the physical and psychological benefits of open water (wild) swimming elsewhere, so I won't dwell too much on them here. Simply put, it can do you a whole heap of good. Any initial discomfort is well worth it: nothing beats tiptoeing into a cool mountain lake, gasping at the numbing cold, and then slipping into the vast body of water and feeling the breeze on your face for a sense of weightless freedom. Then, clambering back out onto the bank, you can wrap up warm, open a Thermos of tea, and let the feelings of elation and accomplishment wash over you. Swimming pools are much the same the world over: a swim in a lake is not – exposure to the elements and wildlife makes it a completely different experience. Every swim is memorable and every one is an adventure.

Alongside all of this come intangible feelings of freedom of movement, the lightness of floating and of being supported by the water, and the sense that you have, for an hour or two, stepped out of the everyday.

Just being in water can create a feeling of relaxation and a decrease in stress, and it is hugely beneficial physically. That 'cold shock' experienced following the initial plunge and which makes you gasp (known as 'the gasp reflex'), whether it's a lake, river or the sea, reduces stress hormones like cortisol and stimulates the vagus nerve, which in turn helps to reduce inflammation and boosts the immune system. Dopamine levels increase to ramp up positive feelings. A cold-water plunge also shuts down circulation to your skin, pooling warm blood in your core. This helps you stay in the water longer. There are further benefits when you get out – endorphins surge around the body, creating sensations of tingly wellbeing and elation.

As for all outdoor swimming, a degree of caution and preparation is key before having a dip in a lake. Make sure you know where you are going to get out before you get in (it is easy to become disorientated or to swim too far), wear a coloured hat so you can be tracked by companions on the shore, avoid swimming alone and don't stay in the water too long: twenty minutes is long enough, especially to start.

When you do get out, beware of 'afterdrop' – the body continues to cool post-swim for up to forty minutes, so wrap up warm straight away and dry yourself thoroughly. (It is also worth noting that the more you swim, the more your body builds a tolerance to cold water – a process known as cold adaptation.)

Five lakes to swim in

The rise in awareness of poor water quality has made people cautious of taking a dip in rivers, but lakes, especially in mountains, when they are spring-fed, are generally cleaner. Check that it is permitted to swim in the lake first, particularly in Wales and England. Thanks to Scotland's lenient open-access laws, it's possible to swim in nearly all its lochs, although be warned: they are very cold all year round. Also check that it is safe to do so with one of the trustworthy open-water swimming associations, such as The Outdoor Swimming Society[2] (www.outdoorswimmingsociety.com), Surfers Against Sewage (www.sas.org.uk) or Swim England (www.swimming.org).

These lakes are recommended:

Llyn Cau, Cadair Idris, Wales: this melted glacier in the middle of the crater of Cadair Idris is reached by an ascent from the car park. Walk straight into the lake from various sloping, stony beaches and enjoy the gin-clear water.

Llynnau Mymbyr, Eryri, Wales: in the foothills of Yr Wyddfa (Snowdon), this lake (one of several in Eryri National Park) is a popular water-sports destination and offers supervised open-water swimming sessions.

Kailpot Crag, Ullswater, Lake District, England: on the quieter east side of Ullswater (there is no main road running alongside), this lake has a beach and a place to jump into the deep, clear water.

Goldiggins Quarry, Minions, Cornwall, England: this lake is inaccessible by car, but the twenty-minute walk to this flooded quarry across the wild and wonderful Bodmin Moor is worth the trek. The lake is fed by a spring, and the water is jewel-bright and deep. Leave the car at The Hurlers car park and stop off at the stone circle on the way.

Loch Morlich, Aviemore, Inverness-shire, Scotland: set in the foothills of the snow-topped Cairngorms and the site of Britain's highest sandy beach, Loch Morlich has a water-sports centre, is the location of various open-water events, and has an inviting café.

---

2 The Outdoor Swimming Society, the go-to resource for all things wild swimming, points out that of 1.85 million outdoor swims logged in 2022 globally, only 207 incidents of sickness were attributed to water quality. Humans are remarkably robust to less than pure water: 80 per cent of outdoor swimmers have never felt sick.

BOOST YOUR OUTDOOR SWIM FOR MAXIMUM WELLBEING

Go for a full-moon swim

Swimming outdoors by the spectral light of the full moon is a magical experience, whether it takes place in an outdoor pool or – even better – a lake, river or the sea. Wonderfully, full-moon swims are also known as 'moon gazey' swims after hares who, when they are out at night looking for food, halt every so often to sit and look at the moon. As always, we should be guided by nature in this, and stop, sit and look at the moon at every opportunity.

John Lewis-Stempel in his book *Nightwalking* describes the 'sheer romance of moonlight on water', and how the senses are heightened at night: sounds are sharper, aromas deeper and vision brighter as it adjusts to the ghostly light. You may even encounter a nocturnal animal foraging for food.

If you are not near a lake or river, or don't fancy walking about at night, some lidos – including Park Road Lido in North London (see below) – hold full-moon swims, depending on when the moon rises and where it is in the sky. Although not quite as magical as a night-time wild swim, these have the power to transform the urban environment into something elemental and bewitching. Watching the light of the moon dance on the waves you create as you push through the water is a moment of transcendence and enchantment.

Embrace skinny-dipping

Slipping out of your clothes and into the cool water of a lake naked is an exhilarating experience: the cool, silky feeling of water on bare skin; the freedom that comes with reducing life to its simplest state: just you, the water and the natural world; the lack of restricting swimwear. The rush of doing something so out of the ordinary and liberating is increased by the sensation that it feels a little bit transgressive. Being naked anywhere outside the home is an unusual state of affairs, especially for the buttoned-up British. Skinny-dipping is a thrill; it makes you feel happy to be alive.

If you are worried about being seen by passers-by, choose a secluded, out-of-the-way place or swim at night, always remembering where you left your clothes… The usual concerns about open-water swimming apply, too (see page 37).

It is worth noting that swimming naked is perfectly legal: you can do it anywhere you can swim. There is even an organisation that runs, or helps others to run, skinny-dips in aid of the British Heart Foundation. For more information and to find an event near you, visit www.greatbritishskinnydip.co.uk.

LIDOS, FLOODED QUARRIES AND NATURAL SWIMMING PONDS

Convenient access to a lake isn't a reality for most of us, especially if we live in a town or city. Fortunately, the increase in the number of people open water swimming has reinvigorated interest in lidos and natural swimming ponds in urban areas. When I lived in London, two of these were lifesavers: Park Road Lido in Crouch End and the Hampstead Heath ponds.

After a day working in a city office and the grubby commute home, arriving at Park Road Lido was like opening a door to a parallel London, a cool stream of liquid pleasure. I would hurry straight there, shuck off my work clothes in the outdoor changing-room, put on a swimsuit, shove everything else into a locker, slip the rubber band with its dangling key around my wrist and tiptoe gingerly towards the water.

Park Road Lido is big – 50 m long – and in the evenings, especially the chillier ones, relatively quiet. It is also heated, although that is not immediately apparent: the temperature can make you gasp. The trick is to get in, push off from the side with the feet, then glide – arms outstretched, head facing down looking at the bottom of the pool so the hair gets wet – into the first stroke without hesitation. Dithering about on the side only delays the pleasure to come and protracts the discomfort. Getting the hair wet feels more immersive and, anyway, it will be wet eventually if you are swimming with your head in the water rather than out, which strains the neck. From then on, as the body adjusts to the temperature, it is bliss.

The size of the pool means that it is rare to collide with the wheeling arms of a backstroking swimmer and that it is possible to really stretch into each stroke and glide, a weightless feeling akin to flying. Clambering out, I would look over at the indoor pool – visible through a wall of glass – and watch the swimmers jostling for their place in crowded lanes in the overheated and noisy space, and wonder why they weren't outside where the air was crisp, the pool was enormous and the stars were starting to appear. My final pleasure was a hot, poolside shower and then getting bundled up in a towel before getting dressed and heading home for supper.

The joy of swimming in Hampstead Heath Ladies' Pond, on the other hand, was that it felt like being in the country, yet it was a short(ish) bus ride from Oxford Circus. The novelty of splashing about outdoors surrounded by trees yet so close to the hubbub of the city never diminished. Once a reservoir, the Ladies' Pond (along with the Men's and the Mixed bathing ponds) is now a much-valued resource for Londoners and can get busy in the summer (it is open year-round). I loved swimming alongside the paddling feet of a duck passing by at eye level as the trees whispered overhead. After a bracing dip, I joined the other swimmers stretched out on the grass bank, sharing crisps, gossip and experiences.

Three other outdoor swimming ponds

Frensham Great Ponds, Surrey: man-made in the thirteenth century as a fish pond, this 50 m wide, spring-fed pond has a roped-off area for swimmers and a beach.

Henleaze Lake, Bristol: it's worth chumming up with a member to swim in this former quarry. Alternatively, put your name down on the (long) waiting list for a chance to while away glorious hours in the 400 m long pond, which is fringed by trees and has lawns to sling a towel on and bask in the sun post-dip.

Lisvane & Llanishen Reservoirs, Cardiff, Wales: book a supervised open-water swimming session in these nineteenth-century reservoirs, now managed by Dŵr Cymru Welsh Water. Warm up afterwards with tea and cake in the community resource café.

Watery Wellness
Blessing the Lake

I was interested to read about water walks undertaken by Sharon Day, leader of the Native American Ojibwe people, and activist, artist and writer from Minnesota, in the USA. A water walk is a spiritual practice which involves carrying water for long distances to raise awareness of rivers and lakes, and to pray for their health. As a child, Sharon hauled water from the well twice a day, an exercise guaranteed to give anyone a deep respect for it. (Women in the Ojibwe tribe traditionally carry and look after water – the men deal with fire.)

One of her events around Seneca Lake in Ontario, Canada, made me think about how it could be replicated in this country around our own polluted waterways. Sharon gathered a group of like-minded women and together they carried water around Seneca Lake in a ritual circumambulation to create a circle of protection. Water was scooped from the lake into a ceremonial vessel which was transported for about a mile by one woman, who then passed it on to another. This continued without stopping from sunrise to sunset for two and a half days. As they walked, the women prayed, meditated, drummed and sang. When they finally returned to where they began, the water was returned to the lake with blessings and offerings.

This strikes me as a powerful way to honour and protect a body of water, and one we would do well to practise, even on a modest scale around our own ponds or lakes.

How to approach a lake mindfully

Although it is easy to drive to a lake, park up and approach it with hardly a thought, it can be a more enriching experience to slow down a little as you draw near. Paying attention to it and to the moment is well worth the pause.

Look at the surrounding landscape and try to understand how the lake was formed. Is it natural or was it man-made? Perhaps it's the result of glacial movement. Can you tell if it is lined with clay or with chalk? This will help indicate what wildlife may be there.

Smell it. A lake in a bad state will smell a little of rotten eggs – the result of bacteria-producing hydrogen sulphide. A healthy lake will have a faint whiff of decaying foliage. Tune into the direction of the wind to help with this – a breeze will carry any smells directly to your nose.

What colour is the water and what can you see reflected on the surface? If it is a sunny day, the water may sparkle with light, and you may see the reflection of clouds. If the lake is lined with chalk, the water could be turquoise.

Enjoy the movement on the water surface. Watch the ripples and see how they move as the wind catches them.

Peer into the water. Can you see any wildlife or aquatic vegetation?

Dip your fingers (or toes) into the water. What does it feel like? What is its temperature?

Set off to explore. If you are planning to do any healing or a blessing, it's a good idea to walk around the lake first, ideally three times, although this will depend on the size of the lake and your fitness. If you are going for a swim, remember to assess the quality of the water and your personal safety first (see page 37).

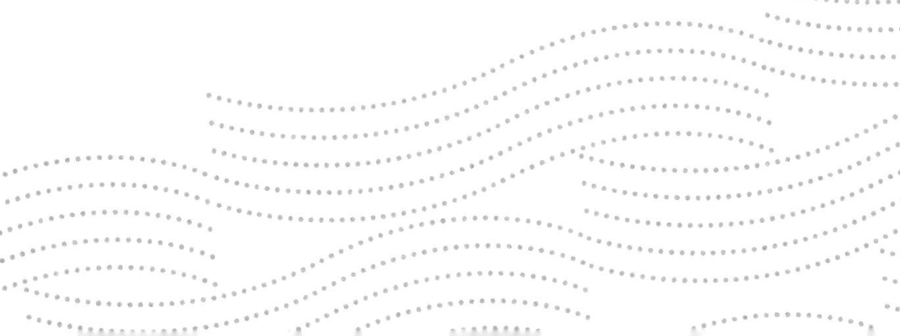

A lake salutation and affirmation

This simple series of movements, based on yoga postures, is powerful when carried out beside a lake (before you go for a swim, perhaps).

1. Stand tall with your feet planted firmly on the ground, hip-width apart, and your hands hanging loosely by your sides. Keep the back of your neck long, and feel your body pulled upwards through the spine and out through the top of your head as though by an invisible cord.
2. Inhale deeply and look out over the water. Pay attention to what you see; the mindful practice above will help.
3. Exhale with a big sigh and, as you do so, fold forward from the hips so that your hands are touching the ground (or as far as you can reach). Bend your knees if that helps.
4. Inhale and come up halfway so that your hands are on your shins. Straighten your back so that it is parallel with the ground and look straight ahead. Keep your back flat and breathe in and out five times. Say this affirmation aloud (or in your head): 'I am flowing through life with ease, grace and joy.'
5. Exhale and straighten up, reaching towards the sky with your hands. As you do so, express your gratitude to the lake by saying: 'I honour you lake, your spirits and your power.'
6. Inhale and bring your hands down into a prayer position over your heart. Bow to the lake.

Blessings From Above: A Word or Two About Rain

Anyone who grows anything, from a pot of geraniums to veg on an allotment, is aware of the value of rain. With one eye on the sky and another on the weather forecast, a gardener is either hoping for more of it or wondering when it will end. Plants, like us, need water to survive, it's a simple truth. So, it always irritates me that when rain is forecast, it is described as 'bad weather', especially in this age of global warming and drought. Storms can lead to flooding and disaster, certainly, but better to think of rain simply as 'weather' which, like the sun, can bring difficulties when there is too much of it.

Rain is not just good for plants, but it is also good for us, and in a surprising way. Take a walk after a downpour and you will notice that everything feels fresh and new; you may also feel refreshed yourself and your mood more buoyant. This is not an illusion: it has been scientifically proven. Rain not only clears the air of pollutants, but it also creates a physical disturbance that releases electrons into the atmosphere. These attach to oxygen molecules to create negative ions. Breathing this ionised air improves the immune response and boosts serotonin levels. The countryside also has a particular earthy smell, known as petrichor, after a rain shower. This is caused by the creation of a molecule called geosmin by bacteria in the soil when rain hits the ground. Inhaling geosmin is also good for us and boosts serotonin levels.

The Three Categories of Rain

Rain is categorised into three types: relief, convectional and frontal. In the UK and Ireland, it is mostly frontal. This is when a warm, tropical air mass collides with a cold, polar air mass, cooling and condensing to form stratus clouds which rain as they become saturated.

Relief rainfall occurs as moisture-laden wind blows inland from the sea, rises upwards and then hits the side of a mountain. As it cools, a cloud is formed, and it begins to rain.

Convectional rainfall occurs on hot days when dark cumulus clouds suddenly appear and douse those beneath with thundery showers. This is caused by hot air rising, and then cooling and condensing until it forms a saturated cumulus cloud.

These are the types of rain I love:[3]

- **A solid drenching** on a summer's night, when you can hear the soil sighing with relief, see plants' leaves bowed with moisture, and smell the clean air and earth.
- **Heavy summer raindrops** that plop into ponds and lakes, causing circular ripples to expand and interconnect.
- **A thundery storm** raging outside when you are safe and warm indoors and can watch it roll across a sky cracked with lightning.
- **A thorough soaking** when you are out walking the dog in non-leaky waterproofs and wellington boots, and don't care how hard it comes down.
- **Rain falling through trees** when you are sheltering beneath an ancient oak, waiting for it to pass.
- **Rain appearing from nowhere** on a summer's day, catching the beams of the sun as it falls softly to the parched earth.
- **The patter of raindrops on tent canvas** as you zip up your sleeping bag, knowing you don't have to get out until morning.

---

3 A person who enjoys rain and rainy days is called a pluviophile.

Blessed be the Rainmakers

Absence of rain has always been felt keenly, especially when life revolved totally around agriculture. If the rain doesn't come, nothing grows, livestock die and people perish. Many peoples considered rain to be a gift from heaven, so devised ways of pleasing the deities – to thank them and invoke pity – to keep the celestial waters flowing.

Music and dance have long been an important part of rainmaking rituals. Native American traditions involve visionary rain dances, controlled by shaman rainmakers, which can last for days and include the entire community. Rainmakers were regarded as important members of the tribe and seen as wise and powerful shamans. In some cultures, they mimicked the effect they wanted to produce – in parts of India, for example, a rainmaker sprinkled water on the earth, pretending to be a cloud, and Buddhist priests filled small holes in the temple with water as a symbol of earth's acceptance of rain.

Watery Wisdom: Animal Rain Forecasters

In some traditions, rain-loving creatures like frogs, snakes, salamanders and turtles were considered custodians of rain. In Central America, salamanders stir when the first warm rain falls in April, and frogs and toads appear when rain falls. Other animals were thought to forecast a downpour. In Ireland, the cry of the curlew and ants scurrying to their hills indicated rain. Crows, geese, swallows and gnats flying low are also indicators. And in Nova Scotia, mosquitoes bite most fiercely before it rains.

Watery Wellness: A Little Rain Meditation

Thinking about rain's cleansing and refreshing qualities is helpful in meditation when you want to let go of something, or release any pain or worry.

Find a quiet place where you won't be disturbed. If it's raining and you can sit outside under shelter or listen to it from indoors, even better, but this isn't essential. (There are YouTube clips of rain falling through forests which make a soothing background sound.)

Monitor your breath as you inhale and exhale. Wait until it slows down to a gentle rhythm.

Visualise soft, warm rain falling onto the crown of your head, then running gently down your face, neck, chest, back and belly. As it moves, picture it washing away any anxiety, difficulties or negative emotions you want to lose.

Continue to visualise the rain moving down your arms, hips and legs to your feet. Enjoy the sensation of it running gently over your body, taking everything negative with it.

Picture all the things you want to lose running away into the ground, leaving you clean and carefree.

Thank the rain for its help.

Dew: a Sparkling Magic Carpet

Dew makes getting up early worthwhile. Step out into the garden onto a dewy lawn on a sunny spring morning (preferably in bare feet), and you leave behind domesticity and enter a small but enchanted otherworld. The usually dull patch of grass is covered with a twinkling coat of minute droplets. Spiderwebs appear as though illuminated with miniature fairy lights. Materialising overnight, then vanishing as soon as the day warms up, this carpet of dew is magical. It is water in its most bewitching state.

Unsurprisingly, there are many customs and folk charms associated with dew, especially if collected on Beltane (1 May), a date full of fresh spring promise, or the summer solstice (21 June), when the sun is at its most powerful. Bathing in Mayday dew is said to bring luck for the year ahead (and to protect you from bad spells), and any dew collected and bottled then can be usefully employed in rituals and beauty preparations. This varies depending on where the dew is collected: gather it from fennel to rub on the eyes to strengthen sight, or from hawthorn and oak to use in the casting of spells.

More prosaically, farmers would create dew ponds by making hollows on otherwise drought-afflicted, chalky stretches of land. The hollow was then lined with clay to collect dew and rain to provide water for livestock.

Chapter Three

Rushing Water: Waterfalls, streams and rivers

'Love this water! Stay near it! Learn from it!
Oh yes, he wanted to learn from it, he wanted to listen to it.
He who would understand this river and its secret would
understand many other things, many secrets, all secrets.'
From *Siddhartha* by Hermann Hesse

Rivers Run Through Us

The nearest river to where I live is the Wye, which starts its journey in the mountains of mid-Wales and then courses along the boundary with England, before arriving at the Severn Estuary near Chepstow. It is a beautiful, wide river that meanders through the broad-leaved woodlands and meadows of the Wye Valley, cutting through gorges as it passes the bookshop town of Hay, the cathedral city of Hereford and the ruined abbey at Tintern. Whenever I drive through Herefordshire on my way to Wales, it is always a thrill when the road drops down and the river is revealed: rushing along, swirling with currents, eddies and ripples, and populated by canoeists, riverbank walkers and fishermen. Yet, like many of the rivers in the UK, the Wye is in peril – agricultural pollution, pesticides, climate change and sewage discharge is causing the life of fish, insects and plants to silently ebb way.

How did it come to this? In early civilisations, rivers were regarded as sacred, valued as a source of drinking water, irrigation, waste disposal, power, navigation, defence and food. Religious buildings were erected along their banks, and offerings were made in gratitude for what they provided and to ensure they continued to flow. Settlements grew around them – they were regarded as central to life.

Until recently, when their pollution has become too widespread to ignore, we barely give rivers a thought. We admired them as we drove over bridges, perhaps, or regarded them as places of recreation – to swim, fish, mess about in boats – but they were easy to take for granted. Even though 3 per cent of land in the UK is covered in freshwater, and two-thirds of tap water comes from rivers, and the lakes and reservoirs they flow into. Ignored until it is almost too late, that is, and we realised the harm we steadily and stealthily inflicted upon them.

To quote Clarence Alexander, former Grand Chief of First Nations people, Gwich'in, Alaska:

> *'Water is a living thing. You have to treat it as such. We don't cuss out the river. We treat it like it's got a soul of its own. This might be our superstition, but our superstitions are pretty much like real.'*

Humans have always interfered with the natural force of rivers: changing their course to irrigate crops, straightening meanders and slowing their progress to create canals, burying them beneath the ground to build cities and funnel sewage (London's underground rivers are a prime example), and draining floodplains to erect houses. While this has many advantages to our welfare as a species, it has sublimated the vitality and spirit of rivers, and depleted the diversity of species found within and beside them. Seeking out rivers and streams that still run their natural course (although altered organically over time) is a pilgrimage worth making. River pilgrimages have history, too: badges of medieval Christian pilgrims have been found at river crossings (and in wells), presumably to make the crossing safer, as well as prehistoric and Romano-British objects.

Making a purposeful journey, or pilgrimage, to a river for solace, blessing prayer and cleansing is a ritual buried deep in our psyches – it is almost a biological imperative. It certainly resonates in popular culture. After Al Green became an ordained Baptist minister at the Full Gospel Tabernacle in Memphis, Tennessee, he wrote about the power of baptism versus romantic love in his song 'Taking Me to the River'; Bruce Springsteen's tragic song 'The River' tells of two young people whose romantic trips to the river and dreams of a better life are thwarted by an unplanned pregnancy. At the end, even the river is no solace; it runs dry.

The importance of restoring our rivers to health cannot be overstated. They are not just life-sustaining, they are soul-enriching. River fishermen know that time spent by a river, rod in hand, is as much about the restorative calm it brings as the number of fish caught. Very little beats sitting beside a river in a wooded valley on a summer's day, watching the water steadily flow onwards, listening to it slap on the bank as a boat passes, catching a flash of brilliant blue as a kingfisher flies low looking for food. Time slips past as easily and as effortlessly as the current.

Rivers induce feelings of contentment, laziness and peace, whether sitting beside them on the riverbank or bobbing along on the water in a boat. As Huckleberry Finn[4] found, 'It was kind of solemn, drifting down the big still river, laying on our backs looking up at the stars, and we didn't ever feel like talking out loud and it warn't often that we laughed, only a little kind of a low chuckle.'

The characteristics and behaviour of rivers mean that they have been loaded with symbolism and metaphor. These can be useful ways to understand life and ourselves: a river's journey from mountain spring to the ocean resembles our passage towards death – starting small, overcoming obstacles, ceaselessly moving onwards until we merge with something much larger. A river makes this passage gracefully, constantly flowing in its search for the sea before tumbling, ego-less, into the vastness of the ocean. A healthy river is restless with energy and movement but, simultaneously, it is unchanging. As Hermann Hesse writes in *Siddhartha*, a river 'is the same and yet new in every moment'.

These qualities have made rivers sacred in many cultures; some, like the Ganges (see page xii), are even seen as the embodiment of the goddess.

4 *The Adventures of Huckleberry Finn* by Mark Twain (Chatto & Windus, 1884).

They are places where baptisms and ritual cleansings take place, and offerings and prayers are sent downstream to reach those who need them. A great river is also a life-giving force and nowhere more so than in the desert. All around the Nile in Egypt is barren wilderness but along its banks there is greenery, life and nourishment. Survival is not possible without it. Consequently, it was a central part of Ancient Egyptian beliefs, and interwoven with the myths and world of the gods, and temples honouring them were built along its banks.

A stream of water moving towards the sea has pools, submerged tree roots, floodplains, riverbanks and vegetation, all providing the necessary food and shelter for a diverse number of different species – all of which makes the tragedy of our rivers' degradation ever more painful. According to The Rivers Trust, there is no single stretch of river in England or Northern Ireland in good overall health.

Fortunately, a swell of protest is building, which offers some hope. Back at the River Wye, a coalition of local groups, Save The Wye, is fighting to save it. Manure from chicken farms, discharged into its waters, has been largely responsible for loss of insects, fish and aquatic flowers, as well as the river turning green from algal bloom during hotter weather. Angela Jones, a river swimmer and campaigner, known as the wild woman of the Wye, has become one of its most vocal protectors. Her understanding of the river and her recording of its decline, built from years of swimming in it, means she is refusing to let it die. As she says, 'I try to play a significant role in safeguarding the river's future and highlighting the decline in species and habitat loss.'

Keeping our rivers healthy and brimming with life is not just essential for the sake of the creatures that inhabit them and the landscape that surrounds them, but for the sake of our wellbeing, our health and our souls.

River Swimming

Slipping into a river then being propelled along gently in its current is a proper immersion in a watery world. If you are lucky to live near a clean river, and can regularly visit for dips and swims, you really get to know it. You become familiar with its resident wildlife, which could include kingfishers, dippers, beavers – even water voles, if you are especially eagle-eyed. Being at water level, you begin to understand how the river courses through the landscape, how it meanders, and how the habitat changes along the riverbank and under your feet. You watch the seasons change and appreciate what that means for the river and its inhabitants. You grow to love everything about it – even the breath-stealing shock of the cold water as you make the first stroke, and the rough, slippery stones beneath your feet.

To thoroughly enjoy a river swim, however, there are certain practical things to consider. As well as the pointers about open-water swimming in the previous chapter (see page 37), there are other considerations. It is important to know what you are (literally) getting into. Each river is not the same; they vary according to geography, activities on the riverbank, geology and pollution. Every river changes with the seasons, too: it may be fuller in spring, faster in winter, calmer in the summer. Rivers in higher rocky ground flow faster, especially after heavy rainfall, which can quickly cause the river to flood or be in spate. This increased volume of water means the river's flow is faster and deeper, and potentially more dangerous. Downstream, the river is calmer and meanders as the landscape flattens but don't be fooled: it may still have fast currents that can whip you along faster than you would like. Watch out where rivers flow into the sea: where freshwater mixes with salt water there are often extreme currents and deep mud. And, finally, many rivers are navigable, so there will be boats about. Wear a colourful hat so that you are visible and don't find yourself dragged under a keel.

To be on the safe side, choose a recommended spot (this will also mean you avoid trespassing). The website www.nowca.org has a useful list of river swims on its website and app. Check for sewage spills at www.theriverstrust.org, which monitors them and charts its findings on a sewage map. First-timers could even play it very safe and start with a guided swim – Ella Foote (www.thedipadvisor.co.uk) is an intrepid outdoor swimmer and has several to choose from.

River Myths and Folklore

'A river seems a magic thing.
A magic, moving, living part
of the very earth itself.'
Laura Gilpin, poet

Rich with symbolism and metaphor, rivers feature in countless myths, legends and fairy tales. In classical mythology, hell had five rivers, which were also goddesses: Styx, Acheron, Cocytus, Phlegethon and Lethe. The newly dead were taken across the Styx to the Underworld by the ferryman Charon, on payment of a coin placed in his mouth. A dip in the River Lethe, on the other hand, brought about oblivion so that the dead would not remember their former lives.

This idea of a river bridging life and death is universal: there is a belief in West Africa that the dead are canoed across the three rivers that connect this world and the next.

Similarly, in Arthurian legend, Barinthus the Bargeman of Avalon used his knowledge of the waters and stars to guide mortals to the Otherworld. He was also credited as taking the wounded King Arthur to the Isle of Avalon.

In the Irish mythological account of the Tuatha Dé Danann people, rivers appear as a boundary between the physical world and Tir na nÒg, the land of eternal youth. Nearly every river in Ireland is named after the gods or, more frequently, the goddesses of that saga (on which, more below/on page 56).

Rivers can be a protective barrier in mythology: traverse one speedily if you are being chased by an angry faery or malevolent spirit and you will be safe. They also had a sinister part to play in the English witch trials of the seventeenth century – women accused of witchcraft were bound and thrown into their waters: if they floated, they were guilty; if they sunk, they were innocent.

River Nymphs and Goddesses

Most mythologies include female river deities, underlining the importance of water to survival – honouring a goddess was a way to ensure that rivers continued to flow. Beautiful female nature spirits (nymphs) also abound in stories surrounding rivers and streams. Many resemble the waters they inhabit, with elegant forms cloaked in long flowing clothes, and a tangle of green hair. Here are some of the most notable:

- **Anuket:** the beautiful goddess of the River Nile in Ancient Egypt. She is usually depicted wearing a crown of reeds and ostrich feathers, and accompanied by a gazelle.
- **Ehuang and Nüying, the Xiangshuishen or Xiang River goddesses:** in Chinese folk religion, the two daughters of the legendary ruler Emperor Yao became goddesses of the Xiang River.
- **Boann and Sinann:** legend has it that the Boyne and Shannon rivers in Ireland are named after these goddesses.
- **Aerfen:** the River Dee (also called Dyfrdwy, which means 'water of divinity') in north Wales was worshipped by the Celts as this goddess.
- **Hafren (Sabrina):** goddess of the River Severn. Hafren was a princess and daughter of King Locrin who, according to Geoffrey of Monmouth's account, was drowned in the River Severn by her stepmother Gwendolen. (Others credit Locrin with the deed, drowning both Hafren and Gwendolen at the same time in retaliation for being forced to marry Gwendolen by his father-in-law.) She is a powerful, mystical figure and champion of the rights of women. There are several statues of her around Worcestershire, through which the Severn flows, notably in Croome Park.
- **Danu:** Irish mother goddess and one of the oldest Celtic deities. Her name means 'river' and is also written as Danann, Anann, and Anu. The Welsh deity Don, who appears in the eleven epic medieval tales of *The Mabinogion* could also be another representation of her. She is also the personification of the River Danube in Germany.
- **Belisama:** Celtic goddess of rivers, lakes, fire and light. The River Ribble in north Yorkshire was known as Belisama in Roman times, although the Romans referred to her as Minerva.

- **The Three Sisters of Plynlimon (Tair Chwaer Pumlumon):** Plynlimon was said to be a mountain spirit (it is also the name of the highest point of the Welsh Cambrian Mountains) whose three daughters 'born of mist' became water spirits called Severn, Wye and Ystwyth. As they searched for the best way to the sea from the mountain summit, they created three rivers.

Something Nasty In The Water

In the poem 'The Green Man's Last Will and Testament' the English poet John Heath-Stubbs warns of nymphs, Peg Powler and Jenny Greenteeth. These demonic, mostly female, creatures lurked in the depths of ponds and rivers, waiting to grasp the ankles of unsuspecting passers-by and drag them to a murky end. It is likely the subaquatic monsters were invented by parents to scare their children from the riverbank and the dangers of falling in, especially if the surface of the water was coated with duckweed, which could look deceptively grass-like and safe. Whatever their origins, they make a terrifying bunch.

Peg Powler: said to have 'an insatiable desire for human life', Peg lurks in the River Tees, north-east England. She has sharp claws and long green hair, which she coils around her victims, especially children who get too close to the edge, to haul them into her dreary lair.

Jenny Greenteeth: a similar character to Peg Powler, this green-skinned and toothed, long-haired hag pulls the unwary of Liverpool and Lancashire from the riverbank. Her name is also used to describe duckweed. Similarly, **Nelly Longarms**, who inhabits the waterways of County Durham, and **Grindylow** are ghastly creatures of the Yorkshire meres, bogs and lakes (and also lurk in the lake at Hogwarts in *Harry Potter and the Goblet of Fire*).

Bean-Nighe (also called Washer at the Ford): a female sprite and omen of death in Scottish folklore. She haunts remote streams, waiting to wash the blood-stained clothes of those about to die. Her cries and screams are carried upon the wind and can be heard by those on the brink of death.

The Ghost of the River Severn

A woman haunts Swan Pool in Redbrook, Monmouthshire, rising from the water while carrying a child. She is sometimes accompanied by a headless dog who circles the pool before vanishing.

Watery Wisdom: Confluences, Where Rivers Meet

The place where two or more rivers merge into one – the confluence – can feel like an especially charged location and is often wreathed in folklore. It is where changes in the rivers' energy, chemistry and habitat take place: a shifting, mercurial habitat full of possibilities. The ancient Celtic god Condatis was regarded as the deity of confluences in County Durham, in the north of England. His name is derived from the Gaulish word 'condat', which means confluence.

Further south, the Mordiford Dragon was said to live at the confluence of the rivers Wye and Lugg. As a young dragon, he was looked after by a girl called Maud, who kept him hidden and gave him milk to drink. As he grew, however, he started to look for something more substantial to eat and began to kill livestock. The local people eventually had enough of his antics, and killed him, leaving Maud devastated at the loss of her friend.

River Pilgrimages, From Source To Sea

Apart from swimming in it, there is no better way to get to know a river than to walk alongside it from its source to the sea. As it flows constantly onwards, it changes, from tumultuous rapids to gentle ripples, responding to the surrounding landscape, which also varies along its course. A walk of this length is no simple undertaking, of course: rivers tend to be long and winding, and rarely have footpaths running conveniently alongside. There will be many obstacles to overcome along the way, from private land to industrial development. (You could take it as a metaphor for life.) Rather than attempt a single long walk or pilgrimage, it is easier to tackle it in stages over a period of weeks, selecting different, accessible stretches each time.

In July 2021, Mollie Meager, an artist in the Forest of Dean, planned a month-long pilgrimage with a small group of concerned citizens along the River Wye. Called Walking the Wye, its aim was to honour the river and express gratitude to it for its life-enriching benefits, but also to draw attention to its polluted state.[5]

The pilgrims collected water from the shore where the Wye meets the Severn and took it to its source in Plynlimon, in the Welsh mountains. It was then carried back to the sea, to complete a circular journey. A series of different pilgrims took the water onwards, with the journey ending on 1 August, which is Lammas, the time of the first harvest in the agricultural wheel of the year. Music, song, silent walking meditation, tree appreciation and picnicking occurred along the way. Meanwhile, the river did what it has always done: flowed towards the sea.

Many rivers have a short journey and are potential candidates for a source-to-sea pilgrimage. If walking their length is too much of an undertaking, a shorter stroll or a mini-pilgrimage along their route, done with the right intention, will do very well.

---

5 With thanks to Mandy Pullen of www.ecoshamanism.org.uk for telling me about it.

Here are eight of the shortest and loveliest riverside pilgrimages.

Afon Lledr, Conwy

Rises: on the eastern slopes of Ysgafell Wen, near Cnicht.
Along the way: the lush Lledr Valley with steep-sided gorge, rapids and waterfalls, Dolwyddelan Castle. The Conwy Valley line stops at Pont-y-Pant station, which has riverside paths to take you onwards, if you want to start your walk there.
Length of river: 16 km
Ends up: merging with the River Conwy, south of Betws-y-Coed.

Afon Solva (River Solva), Pembrokeshire

Rises: a few hundred metres south-east of the village of Croesgoch.
Along the way: agricultural land, the villages of Lower Solva and Middle Mill, a flooded coastal valley, Solva harbour and village.
Length of river: 16 km
Ends up: at the harbour at Solva, St Bride's Bay.

Afon Dysynni, mid-Wales

Rises: Llyn Tal-y-llyn (also known as Llyn Mwyngil), south of Cadair Idris.
Along the way: scenic valley with ruins of Castell y Bere, Abergynolwyn World Heritage slate village, Craig yr Aderyn (cormorants nest here).
Length of river: 32 km
Ends up: at a coastal lagoon, Morlyn (Broadwater), at Cardigan Bay, north of Tywyn beach, after its confluence with Afon Cader.

Afon Rheidol, Ceredigion

Rises: Llyn Llygad Rheidol on the slopes of Pumlumon mountain, the highest point in the Cambrian mountains.
Along the way: Nant y Moch reservoir and hydroelectric power station, a steep gorge through Welsh Oak ancient woodland, Gyfarllwyd Falls, seen through the trees at Devil's Bridge (see page 67), the abandoned workings of Cwm Rheidol lead mine.

Length of river: 31 km

Ends up: the estuary at Aberystwyth, after its confluence with Afon Ystwyth, before flowing into Cardigan Bay.

A legend tells of how a mountain king sent his three daughters – the rivers Severn, Wye and Rheidol – to find the sea. Each took a different route: the Severn rose early and took a long, meandering path; the Wye did the same but was more direct; and the Rheidol rose late and took the fastest route it could, tripping and leaping all the way to Cardigan Bay.

Afon Mawddach, Gwynedd

Rises: north of Dduallt, Snowdonia.

Along the way: many significant tributaries, a salmon and trout fishery, a wide and sandy estuary at the finish. An old railway line is now an 8-mile cycle path along the south side of the river, running from Dolgellau to Morfa Mawddach.

Length of river: 45 km

Ends up: after its confluence with Afon Wnion at a sandy estuary, with Barmouth at its mouth.

Crumlin River, Antrim, Northern Ireland

Rises: eastern slopes of Divis Mountain.

Along the way: the trail takes you along a short but deep glen through woods. You might see otters and herons, and trout and salmon in late summer and early autumn (it is popular with anglers, although there have been protests about overfishing).

Length of river: 21 km

Ends up: Lough Neagh.

River Parrett, Dorset and Somerset

Rises: Cheddington, Dorset.

Along the way: a path created by arts and government bodies is lined with artworks. There are also pretty villages, moorland, the Somerset Levels and wetland populated with wading birds.

Length of river: 80 km

Ends up: Bridgwater Bay, Somerset.

River Ayr, Ayrshire, Scotland

Rises: Glenbuck Loch, East Ayrshire.

Along the way: a disused railway track takes you into gentle countryside, moorland, sandstone gorges, a ruined castle, several villages and farmland. Remains of prehistoric sacrificial horse burials have been found along its banks, suggesting the river was held sacred by pre-Christian people.

Length of river: 65 km

Ends up: the Firth of Clyde, at the town of Ayr.

Alder: Tree of the Wetlands

No other tree loves water as much as the alder (*Alnus glutinosa*). Flourishing along riverbanks and near lakes and ponds, it is seen as the guardian of watery places, protecting the water spirits that dwell there. It thrives in boggy ground, its roots buried in the wet soil, knitting it together and preventing erosion. Uniquely, the wood of the alder does not rot in the water but grows stronger and harder. A woodland that is predominantly alder is called a 'carr' and is usually boggy underfoot, with a mysterious atmosphere. Cut a branch and the pale wood turns orange: in Irish folklore it was considered unlucky because of this and avoided.

Identify alder by its leaves, which are never pointed at the tip but often have an indentation like a heart, and by its catkins: the male are yellow and dangling; the female are oval and green. Both grow on the same tree and can be spotted from February until April. The flowers can be used to make green dye – Robin Hood was said to have camouflaged his and his Merry Men's clothes with dye made from alder.

Waterfalls: Magical Watery Curtains

THE FOUR FALLS TRAIL, Ystradfellte, Wales

The car park was almost full. The attendant instructed me to reverse-park to enable an easy exit later in the day, when it would be at capacity. Usually, the sight of a full car park makes my heart sink, all hopes of a quiet wander vanishing with the arrival of each new vehicle. Here, though, I didn't mind. I knew that the walk to the four waterfalls was reasonably lengthy (5 miles there and back) and involved steep gradients with heart-thumping ascents. Unlike other tourist spots where everything is right in front of you, at Ystradfellte you work for your rewards. I didn't begrudge anyone who was prepared to make the effort and, besides, there was room for all.

The four waterfalls at Ystradfellte rise in tiers up the steep-sided valley of the River Mellte and grow increasingly spectacular as you venture along the trail, ending in the tumultuous and thunderous Sgwd yr Eira on the River Hepste. The trail had the feel of a pilgrimage: everyone on the path had the same goal – to reach the waterfalls, to marvel at the spectacle and to benefit from the exhilarating and refreshing power of the huge amounts of tumbling water. That day, the path attracted every variation of humankind, from solitary dog walkers to groups of children herded along by overly enthusiastic teachers, and young couples on dates wearing inappropriate clothing. The mood was convivial, with cheery hellos exchanged, accompanied by warnings to 'be careful, it's slippery down there'.

The valley itself is enough to enliven the most dormant of spirits. Far-reaching views are framed by shimmering silver birches decorated with tufts of lichen and, along the riverbanks, humps of boulders are coated with velvety moss. I visited in spring, when the river was brimful, newly emerged plants and unfurling leaves were vivid green, and lambs jumped into the air, for the sheer joy of it.

I heard the waterfalls before I saw them, the great boom urging me along, until they revealed themselves – walls of white foaming water restlessly falling.

Waterfalls are the result of water dropping from one level to another, often from a hard rock to a more easily eroded softer rock. They come in many guises, including plunge (a straight, free-falling, vertical drop); horsetail, where the water has contact with the rock on the way down, creating long, thin streams; punchbowl, where water ends up in a pool; and cascade (a series of small falls as water hits rock steps on its descent).

On a sunnier day, a rainbow might appear over a waterfall, arching overhead as light is refracted in the water droplets of the fall's spray. I saw this once at its most dramatic at the Skógafoss waterfall in Iceland. The water thunders down from a 60 m height – a plunge waterfall – creating consistent amounts of spray: perfect conditions for rainbows, which are almost always visible when the sun is out.

Each of the four waterfalls at Ystradfellte was reached by a descent of varying gradients (boots with a good grip are essential) and at their feet, a cluster of people stood, taking pictures, and enjoying the spectacle and the feeling of cooling water on their hot faces. At the final, most spectacular, waterfall, Sgwd yr Eira (a plunge waterfall ending in a cascade), I followed in the footsteps of sheep farmers, who once herded their animals behind the great curtain of white water, to immerse myself in the sound and the spray.

It is not just the visual spectacle that draws us to waterfalls. They are also credited with the ability to calm, cleanse and soothe the body. Being immersed, and sometimes drenched, in water at such a remarkable place connects you to the power of nature and reminds you of your part in the greater scheme of things. Tapping into these wellsprings of exuberant life-force does not require anything of us apart from the determination to visit them (although they can be powerful places to meditate); all that is necessary is to look, listen and marvel.

Waterfalls are also regarded as places to contact the spirit world by shaman and seers from many cultures, and are seen as gathering points for ancestral souls. Sleeping beside one is said to induce prophetic dreams and visions. During an initiation ceremony held by the Jivaroan people of Ecuador, the person to be initiated walks naked behind the waterfall, chanting as they go, before drinking potent tobacco water and waiting for a vision. On returning home, they will dream of the ancestral soul who appeared in the vision, causing the power of that spirit to enter their bodies.

There is some science behind what is called 'the waterfall effect'. When water molecules collide and interact with air, as they do repeatedly when falling from a height (much like rainfall, see page 46), they release negative oxygen ions. These increase our levels of the mood-regulating chemical serotonin, as well as the flow of oxygen to the brain. There are many alleged benefits to this, including higher alertness and more mental energy. I certainly felt recharged and thoroughly refreshed after my walk behind Sgwd yr Eira. If nothing else, it was the boost I needed to climb back up to the footpath and retrace my steps to the car park.

LEGENDS OF THE FALLS

The awesome, magical quality of waterfalls has generated many myths and legends, especially in Wales. Here are five falls that come wreathed in tales of fairies, witches and flying dragons.

1. A greedy serpent and the spirits of the dead: Pistyll Rhaeadr, Berwyn Mountains, Powys

Legend has it that Gwybr, a winged serpent, lived at the top of Pistyll Rhaeadr, frequently flying down to the local village of Llanrhaeadr to steal children, women and animals with a view to eating them for his supper. The frequent murders caused the water to flow red with the blood of his victims. Gwybr was eventually vanquished by a wise older woman who cleverly wrapped a spiky post in a red blanket and offered it to him. As the serpent coiled itself around the post, it impaled itself on the spikes and died. A prehistoric standing stone, Post y Wiber, in a nearby field, is said to be the petrified version of the post.

One of the Seven Wonders of Wales,[6] the falls are 73 m high; they have two drops along their length, four pools and a natural stone bridge (known as the fairy bridge) spanning its width. A little out of the way, Pistyll Rhaeadr still gets busy in the summer. Plan a trip there in winter instead to avoid the crowds, and you may also discover a fairyland of icicles caused by spray freezing on the surrounding trees and plants.

---

6 The others are Wrexham steeple, Snowdon, Overton yew trees, St Winefride's Well (see page 18), Llangollen Bridge and Gresford bells.

The Berwyn Mountains, which feed the falls its water, is said to be the realm of Annwn, the Celtic Otherworld, where the spirits of the dead reside. Waterfalls, like wells and rivers, are often seen as a portal between this world and the 'other'. The area above Pistyll Rhaeadr is known as Rhos y Beddau, the Moor of the Graves.

2. Frolicking fairies: Four Falls Trail, Ystradfellte, Bannau Brycheiniog

The four waterfalls in the Vale of Neath (aka Waterfall Country) are the result of three rivers – the Mellte, Hepste and Nedd-fechan – carving their way through soft rocks to create a gorgeous tree-lined gorge (see above). The area is a well-known haunt of fairies, who inhabit its many magical caves, woods, hills and, of course, waterfalls. It is said that on moonlit nights, you can spot them dancing and somersaulting on the nearby wooded hillfort of Craig y Ddinas.

3. More fairies and a fearsome monster: Rhaeadr y Tylwyth Teg, Trefriw, Conwy

The name 'Fairy Falls' (Rhaeadr y Tylwyth Teg) was coined by Victorian fairy enthusiasts, of which there were many, and refers to the smaller falls that gurgle and splash downstream from the main waterfall. The narrow, fern-lined gorge, topped by the 7 m high fall, opens out to this area of pools, rocks, nooks and crannies: the perfect habitat for fairies to weave their mischievous enchantments. Upstream, along the River Crafnant, it was said that a ghastly Afanc (monster) once lurked in a pool, gobbling up its many victims. It came to a sticky end when a beautiful young woman charmed it from its lair for it to be chained and dragged away by a couple of oxen.

4. A wicked ghost: Rhaeadr Ewynnol (Swallow Falls), Betws-y-Coed, Conwy

This is a popular tourist spot, possibly because it is easy to reach, but also because this cascade of multiple waterfalls is a tumbling froth of white water. It is a little discordant then that it is haunted by the ghost of a most unpleasant reprobate, Sir John Wynn of Gwdyir. A local tyrant who mistreated the locals, his misdeeds finally caught up with him when he was declared a public nuisance and imprisoned. His spirit is trapped in the falls and his miserable wails can still be heard emanating from the foaming water. A viewing platform overlooks the falls, but to really hear the ghost of old Sir John, walk down to the river's edge and listen intently.

5. The Devil his very self: Rhaeadrau Pontarfynach (Devil's Bridge Falls), near Aberystwyth, Ceredigion

William Wordsworth pondered, 'from what huge height, descending' this waterfall fell, in his poem 'To the Torrent at Devil's Bridge, North Wales' in 1824. He was one of many visitors to the waterfall during the eighteenth century, and it is still as popular now. The 'huge height' it descends from is 91 m, with five major drops and, unusually, it has three bridges spanning its width. The first was built in the eleventh century, and so impressive was this engineering feat that it was thought no mortal could have constructed it – it must have been the work of the Devil. Various legends tell of how this came to pass but most agree that it was a bargain struck between a builder and the Devil. In return for allowing the bridge to be built, the Devil could claim the first living thing to cross it. A cunning woman sent a dog over instead of a human and thus his plans were foiled. In reality, the bridge was probably built by the monks at nearby Strata Florida abbey (where it was also rumoured that the Holy Grail was kept for safekeeping on its way to Glastonbury.) The second bridge was built in 1752, and the third, the highest, in 1901.

SIX OTHER ENCHANTED UK WATERFALLS

1. WRAP-AROUND MAGIC at St Nectan's Glen, Trethevy, Tintagel, Cornwall

Seekers of the numinous, healing and magic should head to this waterfall tucked away in a rocky gorge deep in woodland. The water powers through a narrow fissure, then drops to a basin before flowing through a large circular hole to reach a shallow pool. The many votive offerings that hang from the surrounding cliffs are testament to the waterfall's importance as a sacred site.

2. BEWITCHING SWIMS at Fairy Pools, Glenbrittle, Isle of Skye

These deep pools of crystalline blue and green water fed by a series of cascades are understandably popular with walkers and swimmers happy to embrace the cold temperature. The water rises in the wild and dramatic Cuillin mountains (Bla Bheinn) which, according to one of Skye's creation myths, were created during a battle between the goddess of winter and the god of spring. If fairies live anywhere, it is surely in this enchanting place.

3. GHOSTLY FALLS at the Whitelady Waterfall, Lydford Gorge, Dartmoor National Park, Devon

Female spirits dressed in long white flowing gowns are often associated with waterfalls, and nowhere more so than here. The ghost that haunts this 30 m high waterfall on the edge of Dartmoor will save you if you are in danger of drowning. Best keep out of the water, though, and enjoy its roar from a viewing platform as it crashes into the gorge.

4. THE QUEEN OF THE FAIRIES at Janet's Foss, Malham, Yorkshire Dales

'Foss' is a Nordic word for 'force' or 'waterfall', and this foss is the home of Janet, Queen of the Fairies, who lives in a cave behind the curtain of water. (Janet or Jenny is common name for a fairy in the north of England.) She has chosen a fittingly magical place: it is lushly verdant, with overhanging trees providing dappled shade for any swimmers in the deep pool below.

5. A WILD AND LONELY PLACE at the Falls of Glomach, Ross-shire, Scotland

The only way to reach this 113 m high, single-drop waterfall – one of the highest in the UK – is by walking 9 km across glens and moors, before descending into a narrow ravine. Its isolation and the mist that shrouds it (*glomach* means 'gloomy') is what makes it magical. Just reaching it feels adventurous, if not a little heroic.

6. A FAIRY GLEN at the Cascades, Tollymore Forest Park, Northern Ireland

At the foot of the Mourne Mountains, on the River Shimma which flows through the middle of Tollymore Forest, there is this magical place of mossy boulders and tumbling water. Fairies are said to live among the hanging branches, playing in the spray from the falls at dusk. (Nearby is the famous bridge which featured in *Game of Thrones*.)

Watery Wellness A Waterfall Purification Ritual

The thrilling power and energy of water ceaselessly falling can be harnessed in personal acts of spiritual cleansing. If you are feeling downcast and heavy from what life has dished up, or grubby from contact with unsympathetic people or situations, find a (suitably safe) waterfall and stand beneath it. (If you don't live near a waterfall, this works equally well in the shower.)

Pay attention to the sound of the water as it cascades downwards, and observe it glide over your body.

Notice the sound of your breath and the sensation of your feet pressing down onto rock (or the shower floor).

Say this sentence aloud as the water rushes over you, from your head to your shoulders, to your stomach and toes: 'This water washes away all that is not serving me.'

Take a moment to let the thought rise, then imagine the water as pure white light coursing through your body and removing mental impurities and negativity.

Thank the water for its healing power, then grab a towel and get dry and warm.

This is an especially magical thing to do during a full moon: the moon is reflected in the water as well as rising above you in the sky, and the water is sprinkled with scattered, sparkling light. A note of caution: the ground will be slippery and, even during a full moon, the path will not be totally visible. Be careful where you tread as you approach the waterfall, wear stout shoes, and carry a torch.

Be At One with the Flow

One of my favourite ways of connecting to water, and the simplest, is to head down to the little stream in my orchard and put my bare feet and hands into the water. The next time you are by a river or stream, give it a go. Take off your shoes and socks and dip your toes, and then all of your feet, into the water. Take a moment to feel the movement of the water and gauge its strength and temperature – really pay attention to it. Next, set an intention, make a prayer or send love and healing, whatever is uppermost on your mind. Say the words out loud or write them on a leaf, then picture them floating away along the river to where they are needed most.

A Mayan Water Ritual

This is a powerful exercise to do during a period of transformation – coming out of a difficult relationship, perhaps, or making a career change.

Pick nine flowers (preferably the same, although different ones that mean different things to you could also work) and carry them carefully to the river in a basket. Turn your back to the river and throw one flower over your shoulder, while picturing the water taking away something that has been bothering you. Turn towards the river and watch the flower go away until you can't see it. Then repeat with the other eight. Thank the river for its help in removing these stubborn and bothersome obstacles in your life.

Dreaming of Rivers

It is always worth listening to your subconscious, and dreams are an excellent way to start the conversation. Generally, dreams about water represent unconscious emotions, with rivers specifically being metaphors for your current state of mind. A muddy river represents troubled thoughts; obstacles in the river mean obstructions in real life; choppy waters equal difficult times, and calm waters a serene patch, for example.

A river's continuous movement also represents your journey through life, and dreaming of one often happens as you enter a new phase. It tells a story of your inner journey, too, indicating whether you are feeling uncertain, anxious or calm. A dream of a lively, rushing river full of energy and vitality might be a nudge to let go of the riverbank, take the plunge and go with the flow, letting the river – and life – take its best course.

Chapter Four

Taking the Waters

The water cure, the cult of bathing and the pleasure of a long, hot soak

'If you want to understand the teaching of water, just drink.'
Zen saying

I grew up in Great Malvern, in Worcestershire, and, although I was vaguely aware of its history as a Victorian spa town, I was unaware of the number of natural springs that tumbled out of its granite hills. My father would regularly fill a plastic flagon from one of the spouts – an activity that appealed as much to his frugality as to his search for clean water – but I very much took this for granted. So, when I moved back to the area after several decades living elsewhere, its abundance of springs and wells (around 100), and the town's acknowledgement of them at the annual Well Dressing and Water Festival were both cheering and revelatory.

During the festival, fifty or so wells are decorated by local communities, and blessings and performances take place beside them. The best-dressed wells are rewarded with a prize at a Family Fun Day in the town's public space, Priory Park, where there are also re-enactments of some of the Victorian hydrotherapy treatments. Priory Park has its own spring, which has an unusually high iron content, once said to cure many ailments including the useful catch-all 'a weak state of the body'. For a few days, these trickles and pools of water, largely ignored in the business of every day, are recognised.

Although the festival draws a big crowd, the visitor numbers it brings to Malvern don't quite match the thousands that pitched up in the nineteenth century seeking a water cure. Malvern was one of several towns in the UK and Europe that exploited their natural springs as the trend for hydrotherapy took hold.

This rejection of conventional medicine in favour of hydropathic practices was pioneered in Silesia by Vincenz Priessnitz. In Malvern, in 1842, two doctors (Dr James Wilson and Dr James Manby Gully) impressed by Priessnitz's methods decided that the town, with its abundant water sources, would be the perfect location to implement them. Whereas other spa towns offered treatments based on the mineral content of their water (see below), Malvern's water was famed for its purity and it was said to 'contain nothing at all'.

This was the right decision: Malvern soon became a popular destination for the unwell, with famous folk – including Florence Nightingale, Charles Darwin, Queen Victoria and Tennyson – all checking in for the water cure. As well as walking around the Malvern Hills, sampling water from various springs, they subjected themselves to several unpleasant-sounding treatments involving wet sheets, the douche – a huge quantity of cold water was deluged upon them for up to eight minutes – and newfangled hydropathic practices such as electropathy and compressed-air baths.

Despite many successes, water treatments fell out of favour once medical procedures grew more sophisticated and more reliable. Visitor numbers to Malvern dropped as hydrotherapy was ridiculed, with the final nail hammered in in 1872, when three cases of typhoid fever caused by contaminated water at The Malvern Hydropathic Establishment were reported.

Although there is no chance of being wrapped in cold sheets or doused with a hose these days, you can still take the waters in Malvern. Collecting water is a pleasurable thing to do, with the search for the spouts and springs taking you all around the Hills and to many of the sites frequented by health-conscious Victorians. These include Holy Well, with its accompanying well house based on a building in Baden-Baden, which has been a destination for those looking for healing since Medieval times.

Malvern's water falls as rain then trickles through a fractured network of extremely hard rock, which contains very few minerals, and it is this purity that makes it special. (Unlike tap water, which is artificially filtered and can contain additives such as fluoride and chlorine, see below.) Generally, the water, which is tested regularly, is of high quality but certain sources are better than others, and some are not recommended at all. The Malvern Spa Association (www.malvernspa.org) has a list of ones with a good, high-quality flow. The easiest and safest spout is the one in the centre of town, where water from three springs gushes from the heart of a sculpture of Malvinha, a Gaelic princess. It draws a constant stream of people filling cupped hands and small bottles with cold, clear, sparkling water.

Victorian water cure treatments are largely derided these days, but hydrotherapy is still practised, including by the NHS. European spa towns are popular destinations for a healthy break – notably, Baden-Baden in Germany, which is famed for its thermal baths filled by twelve springs, the elegant town of Vichy in France, known as 'Queen of Spas', and Karlovy Vary, in the Czech Republic, which has seventy-nine hot springs.

Watery Wisdom: Romans and their Bath Houses

Although the Ancient Greeks were the first to create communal public baths – mostly for use post-physical exertion and prior to intellectual discussion – it was the Romans who took bathing to magnificent proportions. Evidence can be seen in the remains of their complex and luxurious *thermae* (bath houses) scattered throughout Britain, particularly in Bath with its luxurious temple/bath complex (see page 76). Roman baths were not simply places to get clean: they combined the spiritual, social and therapeutic aspects of bathing, exalting it to an art form. Alongside rooms of varying temperatures, and thermally heated pools, were reading rooms, temples and libraries. This new bath-house culture came with a range of alternative water deities and spirits, which were often married with pre-existing local equivalents. (Later, Christian missionaries gave them new names and allied them to new legends, while essentially retaining their original meanings.) Roman bath houses can be seen as the forerunners of modern spas, although they eventually descended into hedonism and licentious behaviour.

Six Other UK Places to Take the Waters

What we think of as spa towns now – elegant Regency and Georgian terraces with pump and assembly rooms, the setting for many Jane Austen novels – were built when the water cure really took hold in the UK, from the eighteenth century and into the nineteenth. Thermal springs were often 'discovered' by a doctor, who claimed all manner of ailments could be cured by either drinking the water, bathing in it or using it to undergo various treatments. Spas drew the fashionable and the wealthy, who could afford to stay in the handsome hotels that sprung up; they combined taking the water with social events and, sometimes, rumbustious living. At the time, traditional medicine didn't offer a cure for cholera, typhoid or tuberculosis, and it often included the use of dangerous drugs and chemicals like mercury and arsenic, so spas offered gentler and more holistic treatments.

These days many spa towns have been reborn as places of retreat and wellbeing where visitors enjoy beauty treatments, massage, healthy eating, stretching out on a lounger by a pool and easing aching muscles in the bubbles of a whirlpool bath. The ones listed below still have active springs or spouts where you can drink the water, but without the extravagant medical claims of their heyday.

Bath, Somerset: a sanctuary of recuperation and rest

When first discovered, the steam rising from the hot springs in the swampy ground of what would become Bath must have seem miraculous. Pretty soon, however, the mineral-rich water was put to good practical use; there is evidence of human activity around the springs from 8,000 BC. It was the Romans who maximised the benefits of this natural resource, however: from AD 43, *Aquae Sulis* (as Bath was known) became a sanctuary for recuperation and rest, and boasted a temple to Minerva, the goddess of wisdom and medicine. After the Romans left, it remained in constant use in lesser and greater degrees, acquiring a reputation as a fashionable haunt along the way, boosted by a succession of royal visits. These days visitors can walk around the original Roman baths and sample the water, which contains forty-three different minerals, at the Roman Baths museum. For a more immersive experience, book in at Thermae Spa, which pumps water from three different springs into an indoor thermal and outdoor rooftop pool, from which you can languorously view the city through a veil of steam.

Buxton, Derbyshire: rejuvenating waters

Always keen to seek out a geothermal spring, the Romans called the one at Buxton the Baths of the Grove Goddess (*Aquae Arnemetiae*). The spring consistently gushed water at a steady 27°C, and it was around these rejuvenating waters that the spa town grew. Evidence of its therapeutic glory days is still very much visible, from the handsome Georgian Crescent, built as a hotel in the 1780s for the 5th Duke of Devonshire, to the Natural Mineral Baths, situated over the main spring, and the Pump Room where the fashionable sampled the waters. Water is fed to the thermal pool from St Ann's Well, on the site of an ancient shrine, where anyone can fill a bottle from a drinking fountain. (It is also available nationwide in bottles, branded as Buxton Water.) Three spas still offer a range of treatments – water-based and otherwise – in the spectacular, recently renovated, Georgian buildings.

Harrogate, Yorkshire: an air of opulence and escape

The promise of 'absolute cleanliness' offered during the town's heyday as the English Spa, at the start of the nineteenth century, can still be experienced in its divine Turkish Baths. Situated in the Royal Baths (which closed in 1969), its rooms of varying temperatures and a chilling plunge pool will thoroughly cleanse even the grubbiest of visitors. Islamic arches, mosaics, tiled floors and painted ceilings give it an air of opulence and escape which was valued by the sickly rich who came here for a cure, and are admired by anyone now luxuriating, and sweating, in its vaulted rooms. The baths were one of several health-giving facilities at Harrogate. Its water, which contains iron, sulphur and salt, prompted many treatments, including the dispensing of medicinal waters, hydrotherapy and mud baths. Sample the water directly from the source at the Royal Pump Rooms in the centre of town and at the Old Magnesia Well Pump Rooms in Valley Gardens.

Llandrindod Wells, Radnorshire: fashionable promenading

Stroll around Rock Park in this Welsh spa town for a sense of what it was like to take the waters in the early nineteenth century. Fashionable Victorian society, up for the water cure, would promenade here after undergoing various cures at the Pump Room and Pavilion (now a café). 'Llandod' is fortunate to have several different types of springs: saline, sulphur, radium, chalybeate and magnesium. Treatment would involve drinking saline water before breakfast, sulphur in the morning and afternoon, and chalybeate (iron) after every meal, interspersed with regular baths and treatments. The chalybeate spring is now a public drinking fountain so its unusually flavoured waters can still be sampled.

Tunbridge Wells, Kent: a fashionable destination

The spring at Tunbridge Wells was discovered in 1606 by a visiting aristocrat, Sir Dudley North, who was startled by the sight of reddish-brown water foaming from the ground. He was not too startled to drink it, however, and found that it restored his weary spirits (caused by too much drinking and partying). He subsequently declared the chalybeate water as health-giving to all of his friends and acquaintances. Quickly, what had been a small settlement grew into a must-visit destination, attracting distinguished visitors who included Queen Henrietta Maria (wife of Charles I) and her son, Charles II, with a raffish bunch of high-living nobles escaping plague-ridden London. By the eighteenth century, the town was a fashionable watering hole, with high society alternating between here and Bath to take the cure. Water still spills from the well, which is located in The Pantiles, and can be sampled in the summer, when it is served from a ladle by a costumed 'Dipper'.

Drinking Water

Most people are aware of the importance of drinking enough water to keep hydrated, although many of us (about one in five) fall short of the recommended amount (1.6–2.5 litres per day, according to the European Food Safety Authority and the NHS).

Dehydration can cause headaches, tiredness and a loss of concentration; this becomes apparent when we forget to top up our fluids and immediately become cranky and forgetful. It makes perfect sense when you realise that our bodies are up to 78 per cent water, and our brains 73 per cent. Water, consumed in the right quantity, keeps us, and everything around us, in good shape.

One hot summer, I was working in an office in Soho, London, when a pipe burst in the street outside. The water supply was immediately cut off and it wasn't long before things, and behaviour, began to deteriorate. Toilets became unflushable and started to back up. Kettles soon emptied and tempers flared as tea-making became impossible. Junior members of staff were sent off to source bottled water. Anyone who had their own water bottle clutched it and stared at would-be thieves through narrowed eyes. It made me realise how much we take a constant water supply for granted in the UK, and how lack of it can quickly lead to poor sanitation, ill health and general chaos.

We are, of course, lucky to have access to safe, clean water: one in nine people globally (11 per cent of the world's population) don't. About a third of our tap water comes from aquifers, with the rest travelling down pipes from reservoirs, lakes and rivers. This has been treated with a low level of chlorine (to kill harmful bacteria) and, in many cases, fluoride (to prevent tooth decay). It is these additions that have made some people suspicious of tap water, although it is perfectly safe and costs very little. Instead, water sourced and bottled at springs has become increasingly popular to drink, replacing tap water altogether in some households.

This search for the best drinking water is not new. In Ancient Egypt, water from the River Nile was the nostrum of its times, collected in jugs and shipped abroad to dispense its health-giving properties. The trend for drinking bottled spring water in Europe really got going in 1789, when French nobleman the Marquis de Lessert drank from a spring at Evian-les-Bains, which he came upon when out walking. After drinking the water, he declared his kidney condition cured. The town quickly opened its first spa and bottling facility, and Evian water began to be distributed worldwide.

A precedent had been set for this in San Pellegrino, in Lombardy in Italy, where a spring had drawn visitors to sample its miraculous water since 1395 (including, reputedly, Leonardo da Vinci in 1509). Like Evian, its reputation was based on its treatment of kidney problems. It evolved into a mineral spa in 1900, with thermal baths and a casino, and a bottling plant was introduced in 1930.

By the nineteenth century, when taking the waters was at its fashionable height, the appetite for bottled water was steadily growing, and water from many different springs and spas was tapped and sold. Criteria for bottled drinking water was different to that used for bathing. Sulphurous water, punishingly odoriferous when used in hydrotherapy treatments, was avoided in favour of water from mild-tasting, palatable springs. Some contained minerals, others were naturally effervescent, and others, like Malvern Water, were still and mineral-free.

To source your own water from a spring, either ensure that it is safe to drink by consulting helpful websites, like www.malvernspa.org, or use a water purifier. These will remove any viruses, bacteria and chemicals.

Watery Wisdom: the Difference Between Mineral and Spring Water

When faced with shelves of bottled water at the supermarket, how do you know which to choose? The first decision is whether to opt for water in a glass bottle, which can be recycled easily, or in a plastic one, which cannot. Are you looking for a simple replacement to drinking tap water or are you after water with a mineral-rich content? Mineral water is sourced from natural springs packed with minerals, such as calcium, magnesium and sulphates. It retains its natural state in the bottle, unlike spring water, which may be filtered or distilled and has its trace minerals removed. Mineral water comes from an underground source, and any minerals and trace elements in it must come from that source and not be added later. It is also purified to remove any dangerous bacteria.

Around The World In Eight Baths

Most cultures have rituals and customs around bathing, usually in response to features in the natural landscape, such as thermal springs, lakes or rivers. While some of these rituals have a spiritual intention, others focus on healing, relaxation, wellbeing or simply getting clean. They all appreciate the pleasures of the calming, restorative, sensuous and liberating experience of immersion in water.

Eight countries who recognise the art of bathing.

1. Japan's hot springs

The volcanic islands of Japan have around 20,000 mineral-rich hot springs. Some are blood-red and naturally scented with hibiscus, while others are milky-white and foul-smelling. Initially, there was a spiritual purpose to bathing in these springs (*onsen*): cleansing by immersion was important to both Shinto and Buddhist monks, who regarded these sources of life-giving water as sacred gifts from the gods and from the earth, and treated them with reverence. In modern Japan, *onsen* are appreciated by everyone as a place to meditate, meet, relax and wash. One popular *onsen* resort is Beppu on the island of Kyushu, which has eight springs with public baths and *ryokan* (accommodation). It was here that Shinto deity Sukunahiko was said to be cured from an acute illness. Treatments includes being buried in naturally heated sand, steam baths heated by hot springs, and mud baths.

2. Bali's riverbank celebration

The Hindu ceremony of Banyu Pinaruh ('knowledge of sacred waters') takes place on the Sunday after the celebrations of Saraswati, the goddess of knowledge, music, art, wisdom and learning. People gather at riverbanks, waterfalls, springs and the seashore at dawn to bathe and achieve physical and spiritual cleanliness. After bathing, a meal of yellow rice (the 'rice of knowledge') and beans is eaten, a symbol of accepting spiritual knowledge, which can now be taken as the heart has been purified.

3. Cambodia's bathing festival

The three-day Buddhist festival of Choul Chnam Thmey, marking Khmer new year (which starts in April), begins with lighting candles at shrines, prayer, offering thanks for the Buddha's teachings, and helping those less fortunate, and ends with buckets of water (previously blessed by monks) being poured over Buddha statues and each other. Bathing the Buddha is a symbolic practice which washes away bad actions and karma.

4. Russia's wood-fired bathhouses

Known as *banya*, Russia's bathhouses have been an important part of Russian life for centuries. Comprising three rooms – an entrance, a steam room and a washing room – they are popular places to gather in many cities and towns, as well as beside summer cottages in the country. Part of the ritual of the *banya* involves a brisk smacking with a *venik* – a bundle of birch twigs. Traditionally built from wood and wood-fired, modern versions are electric-powered, which means the cantankerous old Slavic spirit Bannik, who lives behind the stove, has been banished. Unless he is lurking in the electric circuitry, that is...

5. Iceland's geothermal pools

Outdoor bathing is an integral part of Icelandic culture, with most settlements having a geothermal swimming pool (*sundlaug*). The constant supply of limitless hot water fills around 170 pools across the country, which are viewed as much as sociable spaces as places to boost health and wellbeing. The culture of public bathing in Iceland goes back to the thirteenth century, when writer and scholar Snorri Sturluson mentioned his geothermal pool, known as Snorralaug (Snorri's pool), in two sagas, *Heimskringla* and *Edda*. The pool, which is in Reykholt, can still be visited, although it is probably a replica. The country regularly ranks in the top three of the World Happiness Report[7] – frequent dips in its thermal waters may partly account for it.

---

7 A report produced in partnership between Gallup, the Oxford Wellbeing Research Centre, the UN Sustainable Development Solutions Network and the World Happiness Review's Editorial Board.

6. Czechia's spa towns

An abundance of mineral-rich thermal springs led to an eruption of spa towns in Czechia in the eighteenth and nineteenth centuries, when the water cure was at its height throughout Europe. The three best known, and most architecturally elegant, are: Karlovy Vary (Carlsbad), the largest spa complex in Europe; Mariánské Lázně (Marienbad), which has forty naturally carbonated springs, and the smallest of the three, Františkovy Lázně, which boasts curative mud treatments alongside 'wellness procedures'. Well preserved, with marble pools, fountains and colonnades, they are still popular places for curative hydrotherapy treatments. Thankfully, these are gentler versions of previous ones, some of which involved electricity, magnets and high-powered jets. Today they are more likely to include whirlpool baths, aroma massage and saunas.

7. Turkey's hammam

The series of progressively hotter rooms that comprise a hammam have been an important feature of the Muslim world since the seventh century. Prayer is one of the Five Pillars of Islam, and it is customary to perform ablutions before praying; hammams are, therefore, frequently sited next to mosques. One of Istanbul's oldest surviving bathhouses, Tahtakale Hamam, which was constructed in 1475, for example, is close to the Rustem Pasha Mosque, although it is now, disappointingly, a shopping centre.

As domestic plumbing improved, hammams fell into disrepair, but many continue to operate for locals and tourists. The majority were built during the Ottoman period (between the fourteenth and twentieth centuries) and are elaborately decorated (this was copied by Victorian England and the trend for Turkish Baths, see Harrogate on page 77). Once progression to the hottest room has been accomplished, visitors are scrubbed, pumiced and massaged, before being left to relax in the relative coolness of the tepidarium.

8. Finland's saunas

Saunas are central to Finnish life, with many homes having their own. They are considered not just somewhere to sweat and douse yourself with water, but as a place of healing. Babies have been known to be born in saunas, and the dead laid out in them before burial. In earlier times, those thought to be possessed were taken to a sauna to have their demons beaten out of them with a *vihta* (birch twig). On 27 July, *Unikeonpäivä* (National Sleepy Head Day), the last person in the house to wake up is considered the laziest and is 'encouraged' to rise with water, using a gentle overhead sprinkle, a startling bucket of water in the face or – for maximum impact – by being thrown in a lake.

Hydrotherapy At Home

Harnessing the health-giving properties of water needn't be confined to spas. Once a few basics are understood, you can improve your physical and mental health with simple applications of hot and cold water in the comfort of your own bathroom.

Water treatments

Hot water: soothing and relaxing

Hot water causes blood vessels to widen and blood flow to increase, relaxing and sedating the body. The ideal bathwater temperature to calm the mind and body is 37°–38°C. (Have a thermometer handy.) This creates a gently indulgent sensation that eases muscles and soothes the mind. It is comfortable to soak leisurely for around twenty minutes in a tub at this temperature. Raise the heat a couple of degrees, to 39°–40°C, however, and the effect is stronger and more relaxing, even sedative. Don't stay in for more than fifteen minutes at this heat, though, otherwise you may become supine and exhausted.

Cold water: energising and invigorating

A temperature lower than body temperature (24°–36°C) causes certain blood vessels to constrict, diverting the blood to internal organs to conserve heat. Many athletes (and some celebrities) swear by immersion in water below 15°C, believing it improves circulation, boosts the immune system and energy levels, and deepens sleep. It certainly reduces blood pressure and cholesterol, and leaves you feeling energised and invigorated.

You don't have to jump into a frozen lake to get the benefits of cold-water immersion. It's much safer, and simpler, to try it at home in the shower first. Start with the shower set at your usual temperature and then, at regular intervals, turn the temperature down for a short burst, then back up again. During the cold episodes, you will feel uncomfortable, then comfortable again quite quickly. Embrace the discomfort: this is when benefits occur. Screaming or whimpering can help, and don't forget to breathe. Extend the cold intervals for as long as you can but no longer than a minute the first time, aiming for up to three minutes eventually. Like swimming outdoors, the more you do it, the easier it becomes.

Alternatively, run a warm bath, get in and splash the water all over your body for a few minutes. Jump out and then dash under a cold shower for one minute. Repeat at least twice, trying to avoid slipping on spilt water as you do so.

A SIMPLE LONG, HOT SOAK

If all you want to do is unwind and relax, the cosseting power of a simple warm bath is unmatched. It can help de-kink any annoying mental and physical niggles that have built up during the day and offers a space to think, away from the commotion going on in the rest of the house. Shut the bathroom door, turn on the taps, involve aromatherapy (see below), light a few tea lights, and in an instant your utilitarian bathroom becomes a mini-spa. No other room has such a dual personality, switching from morning wash-house to evening sanctuary.

To ramp up this sanctuary-at-home feeling, elevate your soak with these spa-time extras.

AROMATHERAPY OILS

The sense of smell is said to be the strongest of our five senses. It certainly has the power to trigger memory, taking you back to a forgotten moment like travelling through time. It can also affect your mood, instilling a sense of calm, sharpening your focus or brightening your spirits, depending on what you sniff.

Introducing certain fragrances into bathtime, with essential oils, is a sensual way to channel this mood-boosting power. I am a fan of aromatherapy because it is entirely plant-based (plants are pressed or steamed to capture the compounds that produce the fragrance), so it is also a way to connect with and appreciate nature.

Don't be tempted to splash essential oils straight into the bath, however. They are not water-soluble, so will create a film on the surface. Instead, either buy a ready-made bath product from a reputable source or make your own. Add between two and twelve drops of your chosen oil (the amount depends on your preferred strength) to 15 ml of carrier oil – coconut, olive or sunflower work well. Certain oils – cinnamon, clove, spearmint and oregano, for example – can irritate the skin, so choose carefully. Splash a few drops into the water after running the bath, i.e. not directly into running bathwater, and be wary of slipperincss when getting out.

These essential oils are lovely for a languorous soak:

Lavender: like lying in a Provençal lavender field in July, with the purple blooms bobbing fragrantly overhead accompanied by the buzz of bees. The scent creates a relaxed holiday feeling, relieving stress and anxiety and helping you sleep.

Orange blossom: this reminds me of Seville in summer, when the streets are heady with this scent. It is warm and not overly sweet; it has a honeyed fruitiness, like exotic nectar: relaxing, sensual, indulgent.

Jasmine: like stepping out into an English garden at dusk, as jasmine flowers release their seductive fragrance to attract night-time pollinators. It can help send you gently into a peaceful slumber.

Eucalyptus: often spritzed in steam baths, this will create the mood of a Turkish hammam. It is a strong fragrance, so blend with other oils if not to your liking: sweet orange, geranium and sandalwood are complementary. You will emerge refreshed and revitalised, with any joint and muscle aches soothed and eased.

Rose: this reminds me of my Bulgarian friend Milena, who always brings me a gift of rose oil from trips back home (Bulgaria is well known for its production or rose oil, extracted from the petals of the Rosa Damascena.) Its scent released into a steamy bathroom will calm and relax, while properties in the oil will soften the skin.

FLOWER PETALS

Bring the flowery gorgeousness of a summer garden into the bathroom by gathering fresh blooms (or using dried ones) and then scattering the petals on the surface of the water. Not only will this make you feel like you are in a luxury spa in Bali or Malaysia, but different flowers will contribute different beneficial effects. Rose petals will soften the skin; chamomile flowers will soothe and calm; hibiscus flowers have a light exfoliating property and good old lavender has antibacterial properties, as well as smelling divine.

CANDLES

The ritual of lighting a candle sets the mood for a soothing bathtime. No one wants to lie naked under a bright central bulb or the cruel glare of an above-the-mirror light. Light a candle, watch the flame flicker bright orange, then light another couple. Switch off all other lights and feel the sense of emotional warmth spread from the flame and into your heart. Tea lights lined up along a windowsill or shelf bring a twinkle to proceedings, and are gentle and mesmerising to stare at as you soak.

EPSOM SALTS (MAGNESIUM SULPHATE)

Confusingly, Epsom salt is not a salt but a naturally occurring pure mineral compound of magnesium and sulphate. It is named after a spring in Epsom, Surrey, where it was originally discovered. It is said to have many benefits if added to a bath, including the soothing of sore muscles and sending the bather blissfully off to sleep (this is boosted if blended with lavender or essential oils). Add two to three cups per bath and soak for at least thirty minutes.

A WORD ABOUT HOT TUBS

I must confess to a minor addiction to hot tubs. I have a wood-fired, Swedish one in a copse of silver birch at the end of my garden which I like to clamber into whenever I can. The thought of the water warming up as I do household chores or weed the garden pulls me through my tasks in a state of happy anticipation. Filling it with water, gathering the wood, lighting it, then tending to the fire throughout the day has become a pleasing ritual. Even more pleasing, however, is stepping into the warm, steamy water as the light fades and the stars come out.

I felt rather smug therefore, to hear of a study by the University of Coventry that revealed that my instincts were right: sitting in a hot tub doing nothing, except watching the moon rise and listening to the trees rustle, is good for you (as a hot tub retains temperature longer than a bath, it is the preferred vessel for this extended hot soak).

The report recommends you stay in the tub for an hour, and that the water should come up to your shoulders and be heated to 40°C. This, it says, will bring similar benefits to those of aerobic exercise – as the core body temperature rises, blood flow improves, blood pressure is lowered and any inflammation is reduced. (Note that hot tubs are potentially dangerous if you have known or suspected heart disease, due to the additional stress on your heart – please do check with your doctor.)

Hot-tub soaking is also thought to be an antidepressant and has been shown to decrease the risk of dementia. I know that I always feel blissed-out when I eventually emerge – a little wrinkled, a little dazed – from the water, and I am fit for nothing except stumbling back into the house and lying on the sofa with a long, cool glass of water, before falling into bed.

Hot tubs are also an enjoyable place to soak with others (although my friend Bridget says it reminds her of cartoons of cannibals cooking up their supper). I can get four people in mine and like to encourage it at every opportunity. Proximity, combined with the warmth of the water and the magic of the night, favours the exchange of confidences and general ruminations about life.

A MEDITATIVE FULL-MOON BATH

As we have seen, bathing is central to most religions and cultures – the spiritual, hygienic, therapeutic and social benefits of water are universal – and is often seen as a sacred act. Performing simple water ceremonies or meditations at home or outdoors, with friends or alone, can be as powerful and meaningful.

This simple ritual, which can be done in the comfort of your own bathroom, combines the cleansing power of bathing with the spiritual energy of the full moon. The tidal movement of water on the Earth is governed by the gravitational pull of the moon, so this is a powerful combination.

Full moons illuminate darkness, exposing shadows in the landscape and in ourselves, and so are helpful when practising healing or self-love. Each full moon has its own name and character[8] (see below), and it is worth noticing which one is rising before you start – it will inform the elements you choose to add or subtract from your ritual, as well as any affirmations you choose to make.

A year of full moons

January: Wolf Moon

The first full moon of the year, and the first after the winter solstice. This is a time of deep self-reflection and new beginnings.

February: Snow Moon

The moon shines brightly on snow-covered ground. All is quiet. This is a time of stillness and introspection. About once every nineteen years, February does not have a full moon. This is known as a Black Moon.

March: Worm Moon

Named for the worms in the ground busily moving through the soil, preparing it for spring. A chance to consider anything happening within you, as you anticipate a return of new life.

April: Pink Moon

The 'pink' refers to the first pink flowers of spring now bursting into bloom. Time to put plans and ideas into action.

May: Flower Moon

May's full moon is all about the eruption of plant life now occurring. Take time to notice all that is going on in the natural world and consider how to replicate it in your own life.

June: Strawberry Moon

The full moon before the summer solstice marks the ripening of strawberries. This is a time of abundance and joy.

---

8 Most of these are English translations of the most common names used by various Native American tribes.

July: Buck Moon

This marks the moment when the antlers of male deer (bucks) are fully grown. Reflect on your achievements in the year so far and on how much you have grown.

August: Sturgeon Moon

This was named by the Algonquin people in the US after the large number of sturgeon fish that were found in the Great Lakes of North America at this time. It marks a time for gratitude.

September: Harvest Moon

The nearest full moon to the autumnal equinox, when the light of the moon enables farmers to bring crops in from the fields late into the night. Summer has almost gone; enjoy its last moments.

October: Hunter's Moon

Deer have grown fat and the hunter is on the prowl, looking for meat to store for the winter. Prepare mentally for the cold days to come, by releasing any negative thoughts that may be lurking and forgiving anyone (or yourself) for any wrongdoing.

November: Beaver Moon

Be inspired by the beavers that are building their winter dams and prepare your home for winter. This is also the time to work with the shadow self, integrating whatever is causing you shame, guilt or regret.

December: Cold Moon

The natural world sinks into slumber as the days shorten. Retreat, rest and be still.

Blue Moon: this occurs in a year with thirteen full moons – when one calendar month has two full moons, the second is called a Blue Moon.

The full-moon bath ritual

Set an intention: is there something you want to develop, such as your creativity, self-love, compassion or patience? Or maybe you want to show more gratitude for what you have. This is the time to put it into words, either spoken or written down.

Clear away any clutter from your bathroom and give it a spruce-up if it needs it. You will want your mini-sanctuary to feel fresh and clean. Have a good-sized towel or bathrobe ready for when you get out of the bath and a glass of cold water to rehydrate.

Have everything ready. This will save scrambling about looking for things. Choose from a menu of candles, tea lights, crystals, oils, flowers or herbs, depending on your mood and your intention.

Create the right atmosphere by turning off electric lights and lighting candles instead. Put on music that complements your mood or intention.

Run the bath and visualise moonlight pouring into the tub.

Put your crystal of choice into the bath. One of these would help to harness the full moon's energy: moonstone to connect with the moon itself; aquamarine, which is associated with the ocean; citrine to help manifest your dreams; fluorite to calm your mind and help it focus.

Add any oils, flowers or herbs that connect with your purpose and the cycle of the moon.

Get in and immerse yourself totally for a few seconds – i.e. get your hair wet.

Make yourself comfortable, ensuring that the water is deep enough and the right temperature. Place a small towel behind your head if that helps.

Tune into your senses. Feel the warmth of the water, smell the fragrance, listen to the music, gaze into the middle of the candle.

Be aware of your breathing. Let it come and go naturally, then slow it down, and inhale and exhale slowly. Let everything you no longer want exit with the exhale; when you inhale, ask for what you want to come into your life, as set by your intention, e.g. healing, love, contentment. Repeat several times.

Visualise yourself outside, under the full moon. Ask it for the guidance and wisdom you are seeking. Stay quiet and listen.

Give thanks to the moon for its constancy and help, and for whatever you have received or hope to receive.

Pull out the plug and as you step out of the bath, visualise negative thoughts and emotions running away with the water.

Wrap up in the towel or robe and drink the water. Make yourself a soothing cup of herbal tea.

Chapter Five:

The Ocean

'Whenever we touch nature, we get clean.
People who have got dirty through too much
civilization can take a walk in the wood,
or a bath in the sea... things are put right again.'
Carl Jung, philosopher

Driving through the winding lanes to Rhossili Bay on the Gower Peninsula (Penrhyn Gŵyr) in Wales, our way was temporarily blocked by a campervan, its roof loaded with surfboards, stuck between a pair of high hedges. We were heading for the coastal path for a day's walking along the clifftop to Worms Head – a most enjoyable prospect, especially on a bright summer morning. Nonetheless, I had the usual stab of envy I always get when I see a surfer. They, more than anyone, except perhaps fishermen, are attuned to the sea. Surfers are in the water as well as on it, spending hours watching it carefully, reading its changes, looking for the next wave. They have what has been described as a spiritual connection with the rhythms of the tide and sea. Plus, it looks like a whole heap of fun.

The surfers' campervan brushed through the hedges and eased its way onward, with us in its wake. I could see the animated figures inside and hear the muffled beat and boom of music. Their anticipation of the day ahead was infectious, and their whoops were audible as the hedges were left behind; we turned a corner and the great expansive stretch of sandy Rhossili Bay stretched out before us.

The sea was already peppered with surfers, sitting on their boards while waiting for a wave, bobbing on the swell, seal-like in wetsuits. We parked up and watched them. Like them, we waited for the right wave to appear. It was impossible to look away until one arrived, a surfer stood up, was swept onto an unbroken crest, rode along its face and then glided towards the shore. It was a moment of poetry and beauty for us, but even more so, I imagined, for the surfer who responded to the movement of the ocean in ways we landlubbers couldn't understand.

Humans have always been drawn to the sea and to immerse ourselves in it, whether as a surfer, a swimmer, sailor or a mere paddler sloshing about in the shallows. Being near the sea creates what Wallace J. Nichols, in his book *Blue Mind*, describes as 'an elevated and sustained happiness, with lower levels of stress and anxiety, a lower heart and breathing rate and a creative boost'. 'Water-associated peace', he suggests, can be credited to the unchanging nature of the ocean: viewed from a distance, it is the same from moment to moment – an enormous body of water stretching out to a limitless horizon. This is a marked contrast to the constant stimulation of everyday life, especially in the city, with all its distractions snagging the attention. Looking out to sea has the power to calm the mind, as anyone who has sat on a beach or a bench, or leant on a railing, looking towards the horizon knows. The sea is mesmeric in its vastness, undulating movement, shifting colours and scatterings of light.

We reluctantly stopped watching the surfers and made our way along the beach, accompanied by the exhilarating crash of waves rolling in from the Atlantic. Towards the end of the beach, before the path rises towards the rocky headland of Worms Head, we came across the skeletal ribs of a ship's bow poking out of the sand. This is *The Helvetia*, a sailing ship wrecked during a storm on 1 November 1887. Gower's rocky coastline has always been a dangerous place for ships: over 250 have been shattered or stranded here during Atlantic storms. Often shrouded by mist or heavy rain, and subjected to ferocious winds, its rocks are a treacherous coastline. St Mary's church at Rhossili even has a dedicated corner in the churchyard for sailors. (Fortunately, the crew of *The Helvetia* were rescued.)

The sight of the shipwreck reminded me that the sea is not always a benign and soothing place. It can be tempestuous and destructive.

This duality, along with its ever-constant, life-giving presence, has led to its long psychological connections with emotions, intuition and the unconscious. As philosopher Carl Jung wrote: 'The sea is the favourite symbol for the unconscious, the mother of all that lives.' (Special Phenomenology; Part IV; Psyche & Symbol.) Both states can be beneficial, however, depending on how each is interpreted. A wild sea can be stimulating and exciting, allowing opportunities to release anger (shouting into a storm as it rages across the sea is recommended), whereas a calm sea can untangle a busy mind and soothe pain, as anyone who has drifted off to sleep on a deckchair listening to the waves can testify. Carl Jung also said: 'I am looking forward enormously to getting back to the sea, where the overstimulated psyche can recover in the presence of that infinite peace and spaciousness.' (*Memories, Dreams, Reflections*, Random House, 1973.)

Our circular walk took us on from Worms Head over Ryer Down to the top of Bove Hill. From this vantage point, we could see the spread of Llanrhidian Marsh on the north coast of the peninsula stretching before us. This is saltmarsh populated by wild ponies and sheep raised for saltmarsh lamb, and it is a vital resource for wildlife and plant species. It was proof that a day beside the sea is not just about sandcastles, ice-creams and dips in the waves. Coastal habitats are rich and varied, ranging from dunes, to heathland, chalk downland, estuaries and lagoons. Each has its own atmosphere, is rewarding in its own way, and worth venturing beyond the beach to find.

Heading back to the car, we could see the surfers still waiting for the next wave. I wondered about having more surf lessons. Then I remembered that on my previous attempt I could barely lift myself from the board to stand up. Instead, I would enjoy the way these surfers surrendered to the rhythm of the tide and the fluidity of the ocean. A wave would eventually come to carry them before its white water crashed and disappeared on the shore to be replaced by another, and another, and another…

Watery Wisdom
Watching the Waves

It is essential for surfers to understand the nature and speed of waves, but it doesn't do the rest of us any harm either. Powerful waves can be thrilling to watch but there is danger in those waters, not just from the waves that crash to the shore but those that surge without breaking, which can be stronger.

Waves are formed by friction when the wind blows across the sea, causing a swell as water particles rotate and move forwards. They can also be caused by seismic activity. The size and power of a wave are determined by how strong the wind is, how long it has been blowing and how far the wave has travelled. The steepness of the slope of the beach and the topography of the seabed will also affect it.

There are three main types of waves:[9]

- **Spilling waves** occur when the slope of the beach is shallow and the waves tumble in fringes of white water. These are the softest and most consistent waves, and they are ideal if you are learning to surf.
- **Dumping waves** break more powerfully on beaches where the slope is steeper. The wave is thrown forward and forms a tube before crashing. These are the waves favoured by experienced surfers but should be avoided by the rest of us.
- **Surging waves** occur when the seabed has a steep gradient. They do not break but are more powerful than those that do and can knock you off your feet and drag you into deep water.

9 Information from www.rnli.org.safety/know-the-risks/waves.

Waiting for the seventh wave: waves travel in sets, with the seventh in the set, which is often in the middle, considered the biggest. This is the wave that surfers favour, as it comes further up the beach and lengthens their ride. It has taken on almost mythic and mystical properties (it even informs a song by Sting: 'Love is the Seventh Wave'). However, the biggest wave is not always the seventh; there may be another bigger one travelling along behind.

The Pleasures Of Paddling

The moment I take off my shoes and step into the sea is, for me, the moment summer really starts. Trousers are rolled up, shoes are carried and the pleasurable business of splashing in the shallows begins. The cooling movement of the waves as they come to shore and lap around the toes is the perfect tonic for hot feet. This is especially true after a long walk, when thick socks and hiking boots are removed, toes are liberated to wiggle and sink in the sand, and seawater begins its soothing and healing work.

Going for a paddle is like a taster of what the cooling sea can offer, and the next best thing to a proper dip. The shrieks as bare feet are engulfed by chilly water and higher waves splash the unwary, are all part of the pleasures of paddling. A paddle along the strandline is also a way to experience the liminal space between the ocean and the land. The horizon is a constant presence beside you, as waves make their steady and constant progress to the shore, their rhythmic rush and drag calming and soothing the mind.

I love one story recounted by the medieval monk historian Bede about St Cuthbert, an early Christian preacher and Prior of Lindisfarne. Cuthbert stripped and waded up to his neck in the sea, where he sang psalms 'to the sound of the waves'. Back on shore, he continued to pray, using the beat of waves as accompaniment, thus creating a duet with nature. A pair of sea otters followed him out of the water and dried his feet with their fur.

Our Polluted Seas

As I write this, red flags are going up on beaches all around the UK coastline, as pollution levels, especially from sewage, soar. Red flags mean that swimming (and surfing) is prohibited due to poor water quality. The amount of untreated sewage dumped into the sea by water companies, often as a result of heavy rain and storms, makes enjoying coastal waters increasingly off limits.

Surfers Against Sewage has been campaigning against sewage discharge into the sea for thirty years. Its website (www.sas.org.uk) monitors water quality at over 450 river and coastal locations, tracking real-time sewage discharge and pollution risks around the UK. Check out its map to see if the water where you are headed is clean enough to enjoy without getting sick. (Wales and Northern Ireland have the highest number of safe beaches.) The website is also the place to learn about this issue, including where to join a beach-clean and how to add your voice to various campaigns.

Estuaries

A shifting, poetical waterworld

Sand, sea and surf are all very well but sometimes you need a watery location that has a different kind of poetry. Somewhere to wander and wonder, a landscape where you can indulge a reflective mood and gather your thoughts. For me, this place is an estuary: the tidal mouth of a big river, a transitional landscape, half-sea, half-river. When in a suitably pensive mood, I walk beside the Blackwater Estuary between Maldon and West Mersea, in Essex: an eerie and enigmatic place with saltmarsh, creeks and tidal islands linked to the shoreline by perilous causeways.

Estuaries are rewarding at any time of year, but I prefer them during the colder months, when the air is threaded with mist and the only sounds are a muffled foghorn from a container ship or the clatter of startled crows disturbed from their roost. In this shifting world of mudflats, saltings and marsh, everything responds to the movement of the tides. At high tide, boats previously mired in mud along its banks and tributaries bob to the surface, their rigging clanking and jingling jauntily. At low tide, mudflats are revealed, providing worms and shellfish for overwintering birds to feast on. If you are lucky, you may see curlews, dunlin and oystercatchers pick their way along, pecking for food.

The squelchy shoreline is also good for mudlarking – digging about looking for historic finds. The Thames Estuary, where the river rises and falls 7 m twice a day, is an especially rich hunting ground. Saltmarsh, where silt and sand has accumulated, on the other hand, is where sheep and cattle graze, and waterfowl feed on the grass, and salt-tolerant plants like sea purslane and golden samphire form colonies.

Although the weather is often misty, there is never a dull day on an estuary. With the variety of views and habitats, and the rise and fall of the tide, there is always something to capture the imagination. But don't take my word for it – take William Wordsworth's, who in 1824 after a visit to Mawddach Estuary, near Barmouth in Wales, wrote in a letter to George Beaumont: 'I took a boat and rowed up its sublime estuary, which many compare with the finest in Scotland. With a fine sea view in front, the mountains behind, the glorious estuary running eight miles inland, and Cader Idris within compass of a day's walk.'

SHIFTING WORLDS: FAVOURITE ESTUARIES

There are around ninety estuaries in the UK. Here are a few of my favourites.

The houseboat community at Pin Mill on **the Orwell Estuary**, River Orwell, in Suffolk, offers an unconventional way of living that looks tempting from the footpath. Nothing tunes you into the rise and fall of the tides like waking up as your home is lifted from the mud at high tide.

The **River Severn** is the longest in the UK and meets the ocean at an estuary in the Bristol Channel, which is also where the rivers Avon, Wye and Usk merge, forming an aquatic boundary between England and Wales. More than 85,000 waterfowl overwinter in the mudflats.

A large part of the **Dyfi Estuary** in Ceredigion, Wales – a magical area of mudflats, river channels and creeks – is owned and managed by the RSPB and attracts Greenland white-fronted geese who overwinter there from October to March.

The whole of the **Helford River** in Cornwall is an estuary (or ria, an inlet formed by the partial submergence of a river valley, as it's correctly called). It is fed by wriggling streams and creeks, including the Frenchman's Creek that was made famous by Daphne du Maurier. Paddle a kayak past ancient oaks, tropical gardens, grand estates, inns and sandy bays for maximum estuary joy.

Birdwatchers flock to Caerlaverock Wetland Centre on **the Solway Firth** in Dumfries and Galloway, in Scotland, to witness barnacle geese arriving in winter. Around 2,000 fly in from Svalbard in northern Norway to feed on the mudflats in the estuary and then fly into the fields at dawn. A spectacle worth getting up early for.

Spectral estuary creatures

The misty, shifting, muddy waters of estuaries are the haunts of many suitably strange and otherworldly beings.

The Mermaid of Padstow, Camel Estuary, Cornwall

Out hunting for seals, a young man named Tristram Bird came across a beautiful maiden and fell in love with her. When she rejected his proposal of marriage, probably for a very good reason, he peevishly shot her, only to discover that she was a mermaid. Her wailing cry can still be heard 'after a fearful gale, like a woman bewailing the dead'.

The Seawitch of Leigh-on-Sea, Thames Estuary, Essex

Twice widowed and mother of nine children, Sarah Moore gained a reputation as a witch in the 1880s. This was largely because she read fortunes and asked sailors for money in return for promising them a fair wind. A local pub still bears her name, and a book, *The Drowning Pool* by Syd Moore, is based partly on her life.

Humber Monster, Humber Estuary, Lincs/East Riding of Yorkshire

This man-eating serpent was said to lurk in this estuary near Hull after a swimmer died there. A large black shape was spotted making its way upriver and was described as having a head the size of an elephant, six humps and flashing eyes. Locals are keen to point out that this beast, seen throughout the 1920s, predates sightings of the Loch Ness Monster and is remarkably similar.

Seawater Therapy

John Masefield's well-known poem 'Sea-Fever' in which the poet hankers for the ocean, has a special resonance for me, as I spent my school days in Ledbury, Herefordshire, where its author was born and raised. It is easily found online or in a book of his collected poetry. Ledbury is as about as landlocked as it is possible to be, deep in the heart of the country and surrounded by soft wooded hills – lovely, but a good day's car journey from the coast. John Masefield must have felt this distance keenly.

Like Masefield, my father constantly yearned for the sea, possibly on account of his years spent in the Merchant Navy. So, every school holiday, we headed to the Welsh coast, which felt like an endless journey in a stuffy car on a hot day. The moment the glittering coast came into view, however, any discomfort and boredom were forgotten. My brother and I, previously fidgety and grumpy in the back seat, were transformed into children bouncing with excitable energy, pointing at the horizon and screaming, 'The sea, the sea!'

The sea has the power to lift the most sluggish of spirits, not just those of holidaying families but anyone who needs it. These days, we mostly enjoy the benefits of the sea by walking beside it, swimming in it or lying next to it, but in the past, 'mind and body' treatment was a more organised affair.

Many of the seaside resorts we visit now, like Llandudno in Wales, sprung up during Victorian times, offering seawater treatments and sea bathing to the sick or anyone concerned about their health. Convalescents with illnesses such as whooping cough and polio were dispatched there to simply 'take the sea air', said to aid their recovery. Bathing machines appeared on beaches, offering sea bathers a place to get changed into cumbersome costumes before being carted to the shoreline by a horse and delivered into the waves. This was not the same as swimming: it was not done for pleasure – most people couldn't swim. Patients spent about half an hour bobbing about in the water, their swimsuits inflated comically with air, in the belief that a cold-water sea dip would 'shock the system' and restore physical and mental health.

Indoors, baths were filled with seawater as an alternative treatment for those not keen on being dunked into the sea. The salt and mineral content was considered especially beneficial for skin conditions like psoriasis, eczema and acne, among others. Treatment using seawater and seaweed is known as 'thalassotherapy',[10] and it became popular in the nineteenth century, especially in Germany and France, where it is still practised. In 1903, marine biologist Dr René Quinton revealed that the composition of seawater and blood plasma are almost identical, allowing the skin of humans submerged in the former to absorb the minerals and trace elements to good effect. These minerals include magnesium and potassium, both essential for converting blood sugar into energy, as well as soothing nerves and relaxing muscles.

This was not entirely new. Seawater has been prized for its health-giving benefits since ancient times: the Greek playwright Euripides wrote in 414 BC that 'the sea cures all human ailments'. Ancient Egyptians used seawater to treat severe wounds and burns, which must have been a painful experience, and the Romans also had a penchant for seawater baths, especially to cure psoriasis.

Today, some spas, especially in France, still offer seawater treatments, while others provide saltwater flotation tanks (see below) and saltwater pools. The support offered by the salty water creates extra buoyancy and can prove beneficial for those suffering from painful joints or mobility issues. There are also many beauty products, from eye gel to mineral mist, that are based on seawater and boast mineral-rich content. Personally, I would rather drive to Wales and plunge straight into the waves at Barafundle Bay.

---

10 Thalassotherapy is derived from the Greek word *thalassa*, which means 'ocean', and *therap* which means 'treat'. 'Balneotherapy' is the term for bathing in mineral water, usually from a spring, as a treatment; *balneum* is Latin for 'bath'.

Floating

A kind of weightlessness

To be honest, I'm not much of a sea swimmer, particularly in the UK, as I find battling with the waves restricts how I swim – I prefer a lake or an outdoor pool. I do, however, love to float in the sea. Being lifted and then supported by the waves creates a light, weightless feeling that is hard to beat. This is especially good in the sea, as there is so much space, so there is little danger of crashing into other swimmers or bumping into the side of the pool, and arms and legs can be extended to full stretch. Suspended on the body of water, head facing up, with nothing to look at but the sky, is mind-clearing and calming – like entering a different time and space. As the ears are beneath the water, sound is muffled so the sense of distance from the everyday world is amplified.[11] The only downside to this most pleasurable activity is the danger of losing track of time and floating away from the beach and safety. It's always best to alert somebody back on dry land that you are out at sea or, even better, swim on a beach with a lifeguard-designated area, especially if you are floating on your own.

Float for life

Floating can also be a lifesaver. It is the best way to get back to safety should you ever find yourself in trouble in water, as it minimises the risk of gasping uncontrollably and gulping quantities of water, which can lead to drowning.

This is how the RNLI suggests you do it (it is also a useful guide should floating for pleasure be your thing):

1. Don't thrash about. Keep calm and don't be tempted to swim.
2. Lean back. Extend your arms and legs. This keeps your mouth and nose out of the water.

11 If you fancy floating on your stomach, stand in shallow water and dunk your face, lifting your head to breathe. Sweep your arms from side to side; then lift one leg and then the other, keeping your hips close to the surface. Remember to breathe.

3. Press your hips towards the sky.
4. Gently move arms and legs back and forth. Cupping your hands helps.
5. Control your breathing until you feel calm.
6. If in danger, wait for help.

Floating therapy

My ultimate floating experience came on a trip to Israel a few years ago, when I visited the Dead Sea with some friends. This strange, still stretch of water (officially a 'hypersaline lake', not a sea) located at the lowest place on Earth contains legendary amounts of salt (34 per cent salinity) and minerals. Even the 'sand' is crystallised salt deposits. No marine life can survive in it.

We gingerly walked into the shallows, then tentatively glided in. The sluggish water did not invite swimming; floating was the only option.

In fact, it is impossible not to float in the Dead Sea, as the density of the water increases your natural buoyancy. All you can do is lie back (with your head up this time – you don't want to swallow that salty water) and relax. Which is what we did, strangely bobbing about on the surface of the water rather than being partly immersed in it, our legs and arms waving in the air, suspended like pond insects.

Many people float in the Dead Sea because of the health benefits of its mineral content (magnesium, sodium and bromide), particularly if they suffer from inflammatory conditions such as psoriasis, acne or arthritis. Others come for its beautifying properties: skin feels silky after a salty dip, especially after being plastered with mud back on shore. We came for the floating experience, which can be replicated, albeit in a diminished way, back at home in a floatation tank.

Also known as isolation tanks, these pods filled with just enough magnesium-saturated water (Epsom salts) to float in can be found in spas and treatment centres. The aim is to create an environment with minimal sensory stimulation – they are dark and soundproof – which encourages you to fully relax. Floating in this cocoon of warmth and silence for an hour or so is said to help ease anxiety and stress, physical aches and pains.

Watery Wellness

A Seaweed Bath

A porcelain bath filled with hot water and seaweed was a popular treatment offered in most large seaside towns, especially in Ireland, when sea bathing for health was the height of fashion in the Edwardian age. The seaweed (or marine algae, as it is correctly called) – usually a common brown variety like one of the wracks – was collected from the shore where it grew in abundance, before being steam-treated to release its minerals and trace elements. It was then added to the bathwater in generous quantities. Patients clambered in to enjoy a relaxing, albeit oily, soak, which was said to be especially beneficial for arthritis and rheumatism. This may well be true, as marine algae contain strong antioxidants and a variety of beneficial vitamins said to help protect the skin against free radicals. It can also aid treatment of skin conditions, including psoriasis and eczema.

Seaweed baths are still offered in some coastal towns: Halen Môn, the sea salt company based in Anglesey, in Wales, offers a seaweed soak in an upcycled whisky barrel, using the pure water generated as a by-product of its salt-making process. Northern Ireland also has several spas where you can soak among seaweed fronds in seawater, while overlooking the shoreline where it was collected. These baths are sold as being good for moisturising the skin, in general, as well as for skin complaints, such as eczema and acne, and for soothing muscles.

To recreate the benefits at home:

Collect the seaweed yourself: look for the abundant brown varieties like bladderwrack and kelp, or dulse, which is red. (Only take what you need.) Put a good handful or two with a couple of tablespoons of sea salt in a muslin bag and drop into a hot bath. Let it infuse the water for ten minutes before hopping in. Adding an essential oil is not a bad idea to make things smell sweeter.

Buy dried seaweed (dulse is recommended) for a less messy alternative. It is usually mixed with sea salt. Soak it in hot water first for around twenty minutes then add to the bath. This also makes an excellent footbath for tired feet.

Sea Swimming

The pleasure of outdoor swimming has already been discussed (see page 36) but swimming in the sea needs a special mention. Those who embrace plunging in our chilly waters and rush into the waves in all weathers and temperatures are evangelical about it, and when they emerge from the sea bright-eyed, glowing and laughing, you can see why. They look elated, joyful and full of life.

Queen Victoria is often credited with the start of sea swimming in the UK. Her fondness for regular dips from her private beach on the Isle of Wight and in Brighton made it a popular pastime: before her enthusiasm for it, the sea was considered dirty and avoided by most. Lidos sprung up on seafronts, reaching a peak in the 1920s and 1930s, until the arrival of heated indoor pools saw them abandoned and sea swimming shunned.

Fortunately, a new wave of open-water swimmers[12] has led to the restoration of many lidos and an increase in numbers of those taking the plunge into the sea – an increase of between 1.5 and three times between 2019 and 2021, according to one report by Outdoor Swimmer.[13] There are several reasons for this. One is rebellion against indoor pools, with their chlorinated water and congested lanes, which I fully understand (see page 40 for my experience of swimming in a city-centre lido). Another is the spiritual dimension of swimming in wild water: moving

---

12 20 per cent annual growth since 2012.

13 Research from Active Lives Survey found that nearly 2.6 million people in England took part in open-water swimming in 2021, also.

in harmony with the waves and feeling the freshness of the wind on your skin or the warmth of the sun on your back. Then there is the natural high experienced, as endorphins are released when your body feels (a short, sharp amount of) pain caused by the chilly temperature. The salt in seawater also makes it more buoyant than freshwater, so it is easier to float and to stretch, as it supports the body.

There are proven health benefits of swimming in water that is cold (usually the case in the UK sea, although it can warm up by September). As you dive (or tentatively tiptoe) in, blood is shunted from the skin to the heart and lungs, which means more oxygenated blood is pumped to the brain. The body also responds as though a mild dose of a virus has entered, causing the release of white blood cells that fight infection, thus boosting the immune system and preventing colds developing.

Most of all, though, sea swimming is joyful. Especially if you join a club and everyone canters into the sea together. Soon you will join the intrepid ranks of Christmas Day swimmers emerging from the shallows, glowing with good health and happiness.

Sea swimming tips

Start with a short swim, i.e. around five minutes, and gradually increase the time as your body acclimatises to the cold. Preferably do this in the summer, when the sea is warmer.

Swim parallel to the shore, not straight out to sea. Then you are within a few strokes to safety, rather than being swept out into the ocean.

Adjust how you do front crawl by lifting your arms higher to miss the top of the waves. Coordinate your breathing with the waves by inhaling between them (which also avoids a mouth- and nose-full of seawater).

Stay within your depth, so that if you get tired you can walk back to the shore.

Wear a brightly coloured swimming hat: it will be the only thing visible when you are in the water.

Make sure someone is keeping an eye out for you on shore. Or swim on a lifeguard-patrolled beach.

Change your mindset. When you first get in, think 'this is so refreshing' rather than 'this is absolutely freezing'. It really does help you get over the initial body shock.

SIX OUTDOOR SEASIDE POOLS AND LIDOS

Set within the shelter of a rocky bay or man-made walls, seawater pools offer many of the benefits of sea swimming but without the perils of currents and waves.

1. Blue Lagoon, Abereiddy Beach, Pembrokeshire, Wales

The sea-facing wall of this former slate quarry was blasted open and purposefully flooded when the mine closed. The original intention was to create a harbour for fishing boats, but it is now a centre for water sports and coasteering. It is also safe to swim here, as the sheltering rocks mean there are no currents, and it is easy to get in and out of the sea. The big attraction is the colour of the water – a striking turquoise – caused by sediment from the slate, which has a high mineral content.

2. Walpole Bay Tidal Pool, Cliftonville, Margate, Kent

Filled by seawater as the tide comes in, this Grade II listed tidal pool, built in 1937, is a great starter pool for anyone considering open-water swimming. It is the UK's largest tidal pool (about four acres) with a depth of around 2 m and walls on three sides – the sea is the fourth. Seasonal lifeguards keep an eye on proceedings. Admission is free and it is always open, enabling swimmers to watch spectacular sunsets over the horizon, like the painter J. M. W. Turner, a former Margate resident, once did.

3. Shoalstone Seawater Pool, Brixham, Devon

This 53 m seawater pool evolved from a rocky cove to a bathing pool in 1896, when two walls were built to retain the tidal water. It instantly became a popular swimming spot, with substantial amounts of rock removed in 1926 to make it deeper, and to create deep and shallow ends. A valve is opened at spring tide to fill the pool. Saved from closure by determined residents who also restored it, it is open from May to September, when there are lifeguards present. There is no entry charge, although donations are welcomed.

4. Tinside Lido, Plymouth, Devon

This spectacular, semicircular art deco saltwater pool is built out into the sea at Plymouth Hoe. Designed in 1935 by John Wibberley, it was a big hit initially but, like many other lidos, it fell into disrepair and closed in 1992. The renewed interest in lidos and local support kickstarted its renovation, and it has been back in business since 2005. It is open from May until September, and there is a charge for admission.

5. Sea Lanes, National Open Water Swimming Centre, Brighton, East Sussex

There are no flumes or slides at the UK's first national open-water swimming centre, which opened in June 2023. Instead, there are six 50 m lanes, with a focus on training and coaching. This is a chlorinated pool, not a seawater one, but the sea is metres away. It is open all year and, best of all for softies, it is heated. Cold showers and lockers are also available for sea swimmers to use free of charge.

6. Newtrain Bay Beach, Trevone, Padstow, Cornwall

This natural seawater swimming pool is hidden among the low rocks that make up Rocky Beach. It is a safe place to splash about in a bay that is otherwise unsuitable for swimming, although it is extremely good for rock pooling,

Whirlpools: Nature's Spinning Spirals

I once spent a few days on Jura, an island in the Scottish Inner Hebrides, researching its whisky distillery. Talk one evening turned to the Corryvreckan Whirlpool, a turbulent body of water permanently spinning in the narrow strait between Jura and the smaller island of Scarba. It had swallowed up many careless sailors, someone said – sailors who had spent a lifetime on the sea. Intrigued, I looked into it further and discovered that one hapless boatman was George Orwell, who was on Jura writing *1984* and got tipped out of his boat by a strong tide emanating from the whirlpool, and almost drowned.

You can see why it is best avoided. Corryvreckan Whirlpool is the third largest whirlpool in the world, up to 50 m wide and with standing waves up to 9 m high. Its booming sound can be heard from 10 km away. Understandably, it is one of the most dangerous stretches of water around the UK. Although it looks like a swirling vortex whipped up by a malign spirit, it is actually caused by a strong Atlantic current hitting a basalt pinnacle on the seabed. This sends water rushing to the surface, where it is trapped by the confines of the strait and turns in on itself.

Many legends have sprung up around this spectacle. Most significantly, it is associated with the Cailleach, a Scottish hag-like goddess who controls stormy winter weather. She was described by writer and folklorist Alasdair Alpin MacGregor as the 'fiercest of the Highland storm kelpies'. (For more on kelpies, see page 35.) 'Corryvreckan' means 'cauldron of the plaid', because this is where the Cailleach is said to wash her tartan. When her laundry is totally white, she spreads it out on the mountains to dry, thus creating winter.

The spiralling of whirlpools, with their constant inward and outward movement, also has spiritual significance. In yoga, the five fluctuating thoughts we all experience, known as *vritti,* are often described as a whirlpool. Yoga aims to still this whirlpool of the mind and stop it spinning. Whirlpools are also used as metaphors in Hinduism to represent the human condition. Those who are caught in the whirlpool are drawn into worldly life, and drowned in sorrow and suffering. They cannot escape from it, unless they become strong and stable by practising renunciation and detachment.

CREATURES OF THE DEEP

The ocean is home to many alluring and dangerous mythical creatures. Mostly female, they rise from its waves, beautiful, seductive and irresistible to the unwary men who cross their path. As cold-blooded as a fish, which their lower body resembles, their purpose is to steal the souls of these unsuspecting fellows. The more malicious among them even summon storms with the sole purpose of tossing ships onto the rocks to destroy both vessel and sailors.

Not all sea witches are entirely merciless, however: some guide ships home or warn sailors of danger. Legend has it that the Devil sent sea witches to help Sir Francis Drake raise a storm and defeat the Spanish Armada in 1588 in exchange for Drake's soul. The sea witches are still said to haunt the land where the battle took place.

Other aquatic spirits fall in love with human men, only to meet tragic ends themselves. The most famous, the Little Mermaid, exchanges her voice and her underwater family for legs and a human soul to be with the prince she loves and saved from drowning. Heartbreak follows, as the prince marries another.

Mermaids

The recent surge of interest in mermaids, which almost matches that in unicorns, has more to do with their seductive beauty than their mythic powers to destroy ships and hapless men. The image of a fish-tailed woman with long seaweed hair covering her alabaster-white, naked form and sitting on a rock, gazing at herself in a mirror, has a powerful resonance to a generation raised on social media. So much so that adult mermaid tails can be bought and used to swim with sinuous movements or to perch on rocky outcrops to boost Instagram or TikTok likes, as a Netflix documentary *MerPeople* chronicled.

Folklore surrounding mermaids has existed in all cultures for centuries. These beautiful creatures lurk along the shoreline with the sole purpose of luring men to their death. The method is universally the same: the mermaid uses her captivating looks and enchanting singing voice to draw a boat or a man to her. Once the individual is bedazzled, she destroys him, usually by drowning. Many of these stories were generated, or amplified, by sailors, who credited shipwrecks, storms and drowning to mermaids' bewitching powers.

Not all mermaids are bringers of doom, however. Some are more benevolent, helping sailors with navigation, or renouncing their aquatic lifestyle to marry a land-born man and raise his children (although this usually ends badly for the mermaid). They are not necessarily female either: merfolk, including mermen, inhabit the depths of the ocean far from human influence, only surfacing along the shoreline to do their deadly work. Unlike the popular Disney version, mermen are often unattractive, sporting green hair and beards, pointy teeth and pig-like snouts. This description may have originated from sightings by sailors of the sea mammal the manatee, which has a large, fleshy form, heavy jowls and a doleful expression, and which could have been mistaken for a half-human form after a tot or two of rum.

LEGENDARY MERMAIDS

Atargatis: the original mermaid

The story of this Ancient Syrian mermaid is one of the first recorded, appearing around 1,000 BC. It told how Atargatis was born from an egg that fell from the stars into the sea and was then pushed ashore by a fish. When she was a young mermaid, she unintentionally killed a human shepherd she had fallen in love with. Distraught, she jumped into a lake to take the form of a fish to disguise her beauty and prevent such a circumstance recurring. However, the water failed to cover her completely, transforming her only from the waist down, and meaning she remained in this mermaid-state ever since.

The Mermaid of Zennor: a rare happy ending

Irresistibly drawn by the sound of bells ringing and lovely singing coming from a church, a beautiful mermaid called Morveren took on human form and came ashore. She entered the church to find the singer was a handsome young man called Mathew Trewella. She instantly fell in love with him and he with her. As she left the church and headed towards the cliffs to return to her watery home, Matthew couldn't resist following her. He was never seen again. Years later, a ship's captain came across a beautiful mermaid singing in the sea. She told him to raise his anchor as it was resting on her house, and she wanted to get back to Matthew and their children. The image of Morveren holding a mirror in one hand and a comb in the other can be found carved into a pew in the church in the village of Zennor.

Li Ban: the salmon-tailed wanderer

When Lough Neagh was formed in Ireland, Li Ban's father was drowned by the rushing water. She, on the other hand, found shelter in an underwater cave with her dog. Trapped, she prayed to become a salmon, like those which swam freely before her. Her prayers were only partly answered: she became half-salmon, half-woman. For the next 300 years she swam through different seas with her dog, who turned into an otter, until she was caught in a net by a monk. He gave her the choice to either live another 300 years or gain a Christian soul and go to heaven. She chose the latter.

Gwenhidw: *morforwyn* (mermaid) queen of Wales

Gwenhidw means 'white enchantment' or 'white spell' and she is credited with using her magical powers to cause destruction at sea. Her herd of white horses (or ewes and a ram, depending on which account you read) ride along the crest of waves on an incoming tide. She was once well known in Wales as a powerful and fearsome mermaid – especially when sporting a beard – and was dreaded and respected in equal measure.

AQUATIC SPIRIT TRIBES

Inhabiting a world beneath the waves, when these siren-like creatures surface, they usually bring chaos with them.

Selkies: seal-like spirits

According to Welsh legend, a selkie was born on land but prefers to live in the sea. They have the appearance of a seal but every so often shuck off their seal skin and surface on land in beautiful human form, usually in isolated places so as not to be discovered. If they marry a mortal, they have to keep their selkie identity a secret. If their skin is stolen, they cannot return to the sea. If a man does steal it, he can force a selkie to become his bride. If she finds the skin again, she can immediately escape back to the sea.

Selkies are also found in Irish and Scottish waters – *selch* is Scottish for 'seal'. Legend has it that a Scottish clan, the Macdorum, were descended from a union between a selkie and a fisherman, and their children were identified by their webbed fingers and toes.

Sirens: seductive songstresses

In Greek mythology, a siren was a hybrid half-bird half-woman with wings and a captivating voice. This was used seductively to put sailors into a trance. Beguiled, they would stop at nothing to reach the source of the song which drew them inexorably on. This never went well, with either the ship wrecked or the sailors drowned.

Undines, oceanids, nereids, naiads: mythological elemental beings

All these sea nymphs are from Greek mythology and share certain similarities. Undines shapeshift into human form to marry and gain a longed-for soul. If they fall in love with a man and he is unfaithful, however, they will die. Like mermaids, they have beautiful singing voices and can live forever. Nereids are beautiful and kindly sea nymphs with melodious voices. They wear coral crowns and flowing white robes, and often accompany Poseidon, god of the sea. Naiads prefer fresh water, especially waterfalls and springs, as do the oceanids, the 3,000 daughters of Oceanus and Tethys, a sea goddess, who are also found in marine waters.

Kelpies: shapeshifting sea creatures

While horse-like kelpies do frequent rivers and streams (see page 35 for more on this), they also inhabit the sea. The Kelpie of Corryvreckan, for instance, is the story of a young woman who leaves her lover for a handsome man, only to discover too late that he is a kelpie and lives at the bottom of the ocean. By accompanying him, she drowns. (Kelpies love to drown humans.) The story is told as 'an awful warning to all fickle maidens'. Kelpies can also summon floods and storms: the sound of their tail entering the water resembles a thunderclap. Anyone who grabs hold of a kelpie's bridle and tames it, however, will have a powerful horse at their command.

Watery Wellness

'Why is the spectacle of the sea so infinitely and eternally agreeable? Because the sea presents at once the idea of immensity and of movement.'
From *My Heart Laid Bare* by Charles Baudelaire

Make a beach mandala

A beach mandala is a kaleidoscopic circle of pebbles, shells, driftwood, sea glass and whatever else the tide brings in. Creating one as the waves lap near your feet and the gulls squawk overhead is both mindful and rewarding.

The Sanskrit word *mandala* loosely translated means 'circle', and mandalas crop up in various faiths as tools for meditation and spiritual guidance. In Hindu and Buddhist traditions, a mandala of interconnecting circles and squares is often embellished with symbols, figures and animals, all focused on a central point. It is a visual representation of the universe, with the divine residing at its centre. Buddhist monks travel mentally through the mandala for hours as a meditation. As well as these intricate and elaborate mandalas, they make simpler ones from coloured sand, which they destroy once finished. This is a lesson in impermanence – everything, however beautiful, will eventually disappear. The same is true of a beach mandala. Once created, it exists for a short period of time, before the wind and the waves wash it away.

How to make a beach mandala

- **Gather your materials.** Take a walk along the shoreline, collecting shells, pebbles, seaweed, feathers, sea glass and bits of driftwood as you go. Try to find multiples of one thing that are roughly the same size, e.g. small pebbles, periwinkle or mussel shells. Keep it natural, i.e. avoid beach litter (although you might like to consider picking it up and taking it home as a mini beach-clean). Find one thing that will work as a centrepiece: a larger stone or shell, for example, or an interesting piece of wood.
- **Find a quiet spot on the beach**. Make sure it is far enough away from the sea so that your mandala won't get swept away as you make it. Look for a hard, flat stretch of sand – that will make the best surface.
- **Draw a circle in the sand.** This will be the outer edge of your mandala.
- **Start working from the centre.** Place your centrepiece, then work outwards, adding smaller, repeated objects in concentric circles as you go.
- **Draw in the sand.** Add embellishments and decorative flourishes with a stick.
- **Leave it alone.** This is a temporary work of art. Let it be destroyed by the wind and the waves. (Although you might like to photograph it to remember what you made.)

AN OCEAN BREATHING EXERCISE

The rhythmic ebb and flow of waves has a calming, de-stimulating effect on the brain. Simply being attentive and listening to it can do wonders to still a troubled mind. Research by Dr Mathew White, an environmental psychologist, revealed that simply being by water has a 'psychologically restorative effect', and is consistently linked with positive mood and reduced stress. Sea air is also full of stress-reducing negative ions (for more on these, see page 65). Regulating the breath to inhale as the waves recede and exhale as they come ashore can help lower anxiety levels further. Your subconscious follows the slow and steady rhythm of the waves, bringing about a tranquil, almost meditative, state.

If you are far from the sea, listening to an app or YouTube video of waves can be just as calming and effective, especially if you are trying, and failing, to fall asleep.

Seaside breathing

- **Sit cross-legged** on the beach.
- **Push your shoulders down** and keep the back of your neck long. This opens the heart space and enables deeper breathing.
- **Breathe gently through the nose.** Make the exhalation longer than the inhalation. Relax your stomach muscles and breathe abdominally, not high in the chest.
- **Close your eyes.**
- **Be aware of the ebb and flow of the water,** and breathe in as the wave gathers for a count of four, then breathe out for a count of five as the wave breaks and rushes up the sand.
- **Continue** for as long as it feels comfortable.
- **Open your eyes** and readjust to the world around you.

SIMPLE SEASIDE RITUALS

1. To release something blocking your progress

Try this if you want to shift something in your life, whether it's a physical, mental or spiritual obstacle.

- **Walk** barefoot along the beach where the waves are coming ashore, keeping your pace slow and steady as you go. As you walk, choose a pebble or shell that appeals to you and pick it up.
- **Stand** still and spread your toes. Be aware of the texture of the sand between them and the seawater washing over them.
- **Look** at the pebble closely, feel its weight in your hand, observe its markings and shape. **Think** about its age and how it might have been formed.
- **Transfer** any fear, anxiety, shame, difficult memory, etc. to the pebble, and thank it for holding them.
- **Throw** the pebble into the water. Watch the splash it makes and the ripples it creates. **Observe** the water washing over it as the ripples disperse.
- **Thank** the sea for taking away your obstacles.
- **Notice** the space now created within you.

2. To ask for something you need

This mindful coastal swim is a simple way to identify what you need most and then how to ask for help to manifest it. It also connects the water within you with the water in the ocean and raises awareness of the interconnectedness of everything, including yourself. To be safe, do it with a friend or on a lifeguard-designated beach, or have a vigilant person on the shore looking out for you.

First, find your beach. Then locate a quiet spot that feels right and where the sea looks tempting, not choppy. This is a full body immersion, so you will need to be in a swimsuit.

Set your intention. What do you want to gain from the experience? What do you need?

Stay present. Listen to the sound of the ocean. Watch the movement of the waves. Feel the sand beneath your feet and the sun (or wind or rain) on your body.

Step into the water. Move further into the sea until your shoulders are submerged, but keep your feet on the ground.

Stand still and sense the movement of the waves.

Allow your body to soften and release.

Look around you, and be open to the experience of oneness and universal connection.

Listen. What do you hear?

Lift your feet and float. Allow yourself to be held by the water. Trust it to keep you safe. (But don't float out too far!)

Mentally release into the waves anything you no longer want to hold.

Swim a few strokes and, as you move, feel your energy expand and your connection with the sea grow.

Ask for what you need and give thanks in advance for receiving it.

Stay out for as long as it feels comfortable. You might like to dive underwater to immerse yourself fully in the sea.

Return to shore and allow some time to consider what you have just experienced. You may want to write an account in a notebook when you are dry and dressed.

THE SOUND OF WATER

It is not surprising that videos of water, from babbling brooks to waves dragging shingle on a beach, are among the most popular videos with insomniacs on YouTube. It is not just the sight of water that soothes the troubled mind and induces slumber, however – it is the sound, at once calming and hypnotic.

Most of us live in a world frequently interrupted by intrusive noise. Traffic and its associated cacophony are the biggest culprits, but building works, lawnmowers and noisy neighbours also have much to answer for. In contrast to the dissonance of everyday life, the low rhythmic sound of the ocean is relaxing and peaceful. It feels akin to the inhalation and exhalation of breath, something familiar and comforting.

The sounds of water are many and varied, a range of volumes and notes, of low frequency and at a harmonic pitch. Each has its own language, be it passionate, soothing or ethereal. Whatever its guise, the sound of flowing water is interpreted by our brains as non-threatening. Simply listening to it can create a meditative state.

Water music

These are the sounds of water I love, with suggested piano music accompaniment. The piano feels like the perfect instrument to capture the sound of water in its various forms. Listening to these pieces of music is as restful as listening to the real thing.

Raindrops falling on the window when I am looking into the street, warm and dry, as people pass by with their umbrellas up.
Music: Frédéric Chopin, 'Raindrops Prelude (Op. 28 No. 15)'

The heavy splash of summer rain falling into the pond after a period of drought.
Music: Claude Debussy, 'Jardin Sous la Pluie'

The gurgle of a spring rising in a mountain then tumbling onwards as a stream.
Music: Franz Liszt, 'Au Bord d'une Source'

The rolling rhythm of waves at sea.
Music: Ludovico Einaudi, 'Le Onde'

Rain pattering through a tree's canopy.
Music: Tōru Takemitsu, 'Rain Tree Sketch'

A fountain scattering water and light in a city square.
Music: Karl Bohm, 'The Fountain'

Further Reading

Books

'Caught by the River, a collection of words on water' (Caught by the River, 2012)

Alexander, Skye, *Mermaids: the myths, legends & lore* (Adams Media, 2012)

Avalon, Annwyn, *Water Witchcraft, Magic and Lore from the Celtic Tradition* (Weiser Books, 2019)

Bord, Janet, *Cures and Curses: ritual and cult at holy wells* (Heart of Albion Press, 2006)

Cope, Phil, *Borderlands: new photographs and old tales of sacred springs, holy wells and spas of the Wales-England borders* (Seren Books, 2013)

Deakin, Roger, *Waterlog* (Vintage, 2000)

Gooley, Tristan, *How to Read Water: clues & patterns from puddles to sea* (Sceptre, 2017)

Havins, Peter J. Neville, *The Spas of England* (Robert Hale, 1976)

Hutton, Ronald, *Pagan Britain* (Yale University Press, 2022)

Kelly, Dr Catherine, *Blue Spaces: how and why water can make you feel better* (Welbeck Publishing Group, 2021)

Koren, Leonard, *Making WET: the Magazine of Gourmet Bathing* (Imperfect Publishing, 2012)

Laing, Olivia, *To the River: a journey beneath the surface* (Canongate, 2011)

Martin, Christina, *Sacred Springs* (Wooden Books, 2000)

Nichols, Wallace J., *Blue Mind: the surprising science that shows how being near, in, on, or under water can make you happier, healthier, more connected, and better at what you do* (Little Brown, 2014)

Pollock, Gerald H., *The Fourth Phase of Water: beyond solid, liquid and vapor* (Ebner and Sons, 2013)

Pretor-Pinney, Gavin, *The Wavewatcher's Companion* (Bloomsbury, 2011)

Smedley, Tim, *The Last Drop: solving the world's water crisis* (Picador, 2023)

Sprackland, Jean, *Strands: a year of discoveries on the beach* (Jonathan Cape, 2012)

Varner, Gary R., *Sacred Wells: a study in the history, meaning and mythology of holy wells and waters* (Algora Publishing, 2009)

Wardley, Tessa, *The Mindful Art of Wild Swimming: reflections for Zen seekers* (Leaping Hare Press, 2017)

Watson, Lyall, *The Water Planet: a celebration of the wonders of water* (Crown, 1988)

Wildwood, Rob, *Magical Britain, 650 Enchanted and Mystical Sites* (Wild Things Publishing, 2022)

Williams, Hugh, *The Mystery of Mercia II* (Lulu, 2022)

Websites

www.atlasobscura.com: a guide to the world's hidden wonders.

www.britishdowsers.org (British Society of Dowsers): charity promoting dowsing in the UK and beyond.

www.druidry.org: the website of the Order of Bards, Ovates and Druids.

www.insearchofholywellsandhealingsprings.com: explores the folklore, history and mystery of ancient water supplies.

www.landoflegends.wales: a story map of Wales to inspire visits to the country's literary and cultural destinations.

www.megalithic.co.uk: a directory of UK ancient sites, generated by voluntary contributions.

www.nowca.org: UK network of safe open-water swimming destinations.

www.outdoorswimmingsociety.com: the go-to resource for open-water swimmers.

www.theriverstrust.org: a conservation organisation working to help rivers thrive again.

www.sas.org.uk: website of marine conservation charity Surfers Against Sewage

www.themodernantiquarian.com: website based on Julian Cope's guidebooks to ancient sites, *The Modern Antiquarian* and *The Megalithic European*

www.wellhopper.wales: explores the ancient holy wells and healing wells of north Wales

Acknowledgements

Kate Smart and Malvern Dowsers for inspiration and help. Guy Hayward of British Pilgrimage Trust for pointing me in the right direction. Camilla Goddard for excellent company on holy-well adventures.